DARE TO SUCCEED

New International Version

Presented by
Van Crouch Communications

Unless otherwise indicated, all Scripture quotations in Part I are taken from the *King James Version* of the Bible.

Scripture quotations in Part III are taken from the *Holy Bible, New International Version* ®. NIV ®. Copyright © 1973, 1978, 1984 by International Bible Society. Used by permission of Zondervan Publishing House. All rights reserved.

Unless otherwise indicated, all Scripture quotations in Part V are taken from the *King James Version* of the Bible.

Scripture quotations in Part V marked NIV are taken from the Holy Bible, *New International Version* ®. NIV ®. Copyright © 1973, 1978, 1984 by International Bible Society. Used by permission of Zondervan Publishing House. All rights reserved.

3rd Printing
Over 17,000 in Print

Dare To Succeed —
New International Version
ISBN 1-56292-042-1
Presented by Van Crouch Communications
1137 Wheaton Oaks Drive
Wheaton, Illinois 60187

Copyright © 1994 by Honor Books
P. O. Box 55388
Tulsa, Oklahoma 74155-1388

Presented to

_____

By

_____

Date

_____

Occasion

_____

CONTENTS

INTRODUCTION

This book was created especially for you. It is specifically designed to provide you with the means to gain wisdom, motivation and inspiration, to set goals and to achieve them — and for what purpose? To help you daily in your career and throughout your life!

In the last few years, life has become increasingly hurried and confused. Rapidly changing technology, a fluctuating economy, political upheaval around the world, wars and threats of wars have caused many people to have difficulty just making sense of life, much less succeeding in it. But God wants each of us to succeed — in our careers, our lives, our daily walk with Him. For this reason, we have published *Dare To Succeed*; we want the power of the Scriptures, the earnestness of special prayers, the wisdom of renowned leaders and the teachings of learned scholars and teachers to be a blessing to you — one that will help you find success in your career and life.

The book is divided into six parts. Each part contains a different kind of information to help and inspire you to dare to succeed. Here is a brief description and guide to using each part.

Part 1 is a collection of motivational teachings from noted authors Og Mandino, Van

Crouch and R. Henry Migliore. Each gives his own distinct perspective on just what it takes to succeed.

Part 2 contains a special collection of Scriptures. These deal primarily with two different areas in your life — successful relationships with God and with others, and with having your needs met.

Part 3 contains powerful prayers for your life. Salvation, commitment, career and relationships are all covered.

Part 4 is a 31-day devotional by John Mason. This will give you daily encouragement and show you how to find the success in life that you need.

Part 5 contains both informational and inspirational remarks about life and living from leaders in a variety of fields — Winston Churchill to John Wooden, Will Rogers to J. C. Penney.

Do as God wants you to do — *Dare To Succeed.*

Part I
Motivation and Guidance

1

Ancient Wisdom for Today
by
Og Mandino

I will live this day as if it is my last. And what shall I do with this last precious day which remains in my keeping? First, I will seal up its container of life so that not one drop spills itself upon the sand. I will waste not a moment mourning yesterday's misfortunes, yesterday's defeats, yesterday's aches of the heart, for why should I throw good after bad?

Can sand flow upward in the hour glass? Will the sun rise where it sets and set where it rises? Can I relive the errors of yesterday and right them? Can I call back yesterday's wounds and make them whole? Can I become younger than yesterday? Can I take back the evil that was spoken, the blows that were struck, the pain that was caused? No. Yesterday is buried forever and I will think of it no more.

I will live this day as if it is my last.

And what then shall I do? Forgetting yesterday neither will I think of tomorrow. Why should I throw *now* after *maybe*? Can tomorrow's sand flow through the glass before today's? Will the sun rise twice this morning? Can I perform tomorrow's deeds while standing in today's path? Can I place tomorrow's gold in today's purse? Can tomorrow's child be born today? Can tomorrow's death cast its shadow backward and darken today's joy? Should I torment myself with problems that may never come to pass? No! Tomorrow lies buried with yesterday, and I will think of it no more.

I will live this day as if it is my last.

This day is all I have and these hours are now my eternity. I greet this sunrise with cries of joy as a prisoner who is reprieved from death. I lift mine arms with thanks for this priceless gift of a new day. So too, I will beat upon my heart with gratitude as I consider all who greeted yesterday's sunrise who are no longer with the living today. I am indeed a fortunate man and today's hours are but a bonus, undeserved. Why have I been allowed to live this extra day when others, far better than I, have departed? Is it that they have accomplished their purpose while mine is yet to be achieved? Is this another opportunity for me to become the man I know I can be? Is there a purpose in nature? Is this my day to excel?

I will live this day as if it is my last.

I have but one life and life is naught but a measurement of time. When I waste one I destroy the other. If I waste today I destroy the last page of my life. Therefore, each hour of this day will I cherish for it can never return. It cannot be banked today to be withdrawn on the morrow, for who can trap the wind? Each minute of this day will I grasp with both hands and fondle with love for its value is beyond price. What dying man can purchase another breath though he willingly give all his gold? What price dare I place on the hours ahead? I will make them priceless!

I will live this day as if it is my last.

I will avoid with fury the killers of time. Procrastination I will destroy with action; doubt I will bury under faith; fear I will dismember with confidence. Where there are idle mouths I will listen not; where there are idle hands I will linger not; where there are idle bodies I will visit not. Henceforth I know that to court idleness is to steal food, clothing, and warmth from those I love. I am not a thief. I am a man of love and today is my last chance to prove my love and my greatness.

I will live this day as if it is my last.

The duties of today I shall fulfill today. Today I shall fondle my children while they are young; tomorrow they will be gone, and so will I. Today I shall embrace my woman with sweet kisses; tomorrow she will be gone, and so will I. Today I shall lift up a friend in need; tomorrow he will no longer cry for help, nor will I hear his cries. Today I shall give myself in sacrifice and work; tomorrow I will have nothing to give, and there will be none to receive.

I will live this day as if it is my last.

And if it is my last, it will be my greatest monument. This day I will make the best day of my life. This day I will drink every minute to its full. I will savor its taste and give thanks. I will make every hour count and each minute I will trade only for something of value. I will labor harder than ever before and push my muscles until they cry for relief, and then I will continue. I will make more calls than ever before. I will sell more goods than ever before. I will earn more gold than ever before. Each minute of today will be more fruitful than hours of yesterday. My last must be my best.

I will live this day as if it is my last.

And if it is not, I shall fall to my knees and give thanks.

Endnote

This entire chapter is from *The Greatest Salesman In The World*, "The Scroll Marked V," (New York: Bantam Books, 1985), pp. 73-77. Used by permission.

2
CAUTION:
CONSTRUCTION WORK AHEAD[1]
by
Van Crouch

Where there is no vision, the people perish.

— Proverbs 29:18

The two basics for personal success are:

1) A *vision* — "a mental sight, dream, or revelation."

2) A *commitment to the vision.*

Exactly what is a vision?

A vision, or a goal, provides specific direction. Without a vision, you *have* no direction. To achieve, you must have an idea of what you want to achieve.

If you don't know where you are going, you will probably wind up somewhere else.[2]

— David Campbell

When I grew up, our home was not run like "Leave It to Beaver" or "Father Knows Best." How thankful I am today for a Christian mother who knew how to stay in the game on her knees before the Lord, praying for me. It made a tremendous difference not only in my life but in my brother's life as well.

One of the earliest examples of a vision and goal was when I got involved in high school football in my hometown of Grove City, Pennsylvania. A man named Dick Bestwick came to coach football. He became a legend. Presently he is athletic director at the University of South Carolina.

His practices were endurance contests. They were hard, hot, dirty and tough. Playing a game was almost like taking a night off. He built a tremendous winning record. More important, Bestwick and his staff worked to build character. He taught what it is to win, to be honest, to give our best. Class attendance was not optional, and respect for parents was a must.

At times, we referred to Coach Bestwick's office as a pool table. If it was necessary for him to call you in, he was likely to grab you by the shirt and bounce you off all four walls. As an educator and coach, he cared enough to confront.

As young men, we learned if we would choose to be tough on ourselves, life would be easier on us. It has always made a positive difference in my life when I have someone to be accountable to. Sound leadership will cause you to develop a vision and rise to a higher level.

Many people today, including Christians, have no vision. They do not know where they are going in life.

As I often say when I speak, the mortality rate in America is running one out of one. Everyone will die sometime.

I used to tell my prospects, "John, when they back the hearse up to the front door, they are not making a practice run!"

Therefore, it is important to make a quality decision to make the best of your life — to be the best you can, not only for Jesus, if you are a Christian, but for personal fulfillment.

Many of us run our lives as Alice did her trip through "Wonderland." If we "do not care much where" we end up, we just keep wandering around.

People with no purpose in life never get anywhere. He who expects little will not be disappointed!

Destiny is not a matter of chance; it is a matter of choice.

A goal gives you a specific direction to work toward.

Specific direction will keep you from wasting effort and time.

If your goal is to get from one city to another, you do not go off in some other direction and wander around, but proceed on course as quickly as possible. Wandering around makes you unstable, or double-minded. Then you will be like the waves of the sea, tossed to and fro, and will not receive anything when you pray. (James 1:7, 8.)

Knowing your destination is half the journey.[3]

In *See You at the Top*, Zig Ziglar says:

"Do most people have goals? Apparently not. You can stop a hundred young men on any street and ask each one, 'What are you doing that will absolutely guarantee your failure in life?'

"After recovering from their initial shock, each one will probably say, 'What do you mean, what am I doing to guarantee my failure? I'm working for success.'

"Tragically, most of them think they are, but . . . if we follow those hundred young men until they are sixty-five years old, only five of them will have achieved financial security. Only one will be wealthy. You can get better odds than that in Las Vegas. . . . Do the people in life who don't succeed actually plan to fail? I don't think so. The problem is they don't plan *anything*."[4]

Happiness, wealth, and success are by-products of goal setting; they cannot be the goal themselves."[5]

Three Reasons Why Visions and Goals Are Necessary

1. They provide purpose and motivation.

2. They provide specific direction.

3. They keep you single-minded on accomplishment.

In the area of purpose and motivation, having a goal and vision to work toward, to attain, will keep you motivated. If people lose motivation and purpose, they usually die fairly quickly afterwards. Also, many times, people *die* on the inside before their bodies die. They rust out before they wear out.

When I came home from work one night, my son asked, "Dad, what have you been doing all day?"

I said, "Nothing much."

He said, "Well, how did you know when you were finished?"

My son was right! Without specific direction, you do not know which way to go nor when you have arrived. Having a vision and a goal will give you that direction.

The poorest man is not he who is without a cent, but he who is without a dream.[6]

— Pennsylvania School Journal

When asked how he climbed Mt. Everest, suppose Sir Edmond Hillary replied:

"I don't know. The missus and I just went out for a walk one afternoon, and before we knew it, there we were at the top.

Of course, that is *not* how Sir Edmund Hillary became the first man to reach the top of Mt. Everest. He had a vision: to be the first man to achieve this climb. And he had a goal: to reach the top of the mountain that had been called impossible to climb.

To achieve his vision and goal required planning, getting together supplies and equipment, finding a guide, and putting together a team. More importantly, however, it took sticking to the job at hand, persevering toward his vision and goal. Ziglar also wrote:

"Do you have a target or a goal? You must have a goal because it's just as difficult to reach a destination you don't have as it is to come back from a place where you've never been."[7]

The Apostle Paul said in Philippians 3:14 that he was pressing on toward the mark of the high calling.

He was saying, "I keep going for the goal to fulfill the vision. I keep the goal in front of me."

A goal and vision will keep you single-minded. For example, if you need money, you should set a specific amount as a goal and a specific date by which to reach that goal. A goal cannot be set for some nebulous time in the future. It must be specific and direct, and there needs to be a deadline.

Single-mindedness is a sign of excellence because it is the single-minded person who wins. He works in a specific direction to accomplish his goal. People with a poor sense of direction in life often get lazy.

Not having a goal results in no direction, but too *many* goals result in a lack of single-mindedness. Being overextended means being tired all the time.

Inspirational Dissatisfaction

Fortunately, I was blessed with a quality I call *inspirational dissatisfaction*. Not being satisfied with where I was, I could believe in my heart there was something bigger and better and move on from there.

Charles Jones in his best-selling book, *Life Is Tremendous*, said:

"The real work is not hard work or difficult work or the actual functions that we perform, the real work is to get excited about your work and that takes work."[8]

In order to become excited about your work, you must be excited about your goal.

The greatest limitations in life are self-imposed. So go for it!

"There's no such thing as coulda, shoulda and woulda. If you shoulda and coulda, you woulda done it."

> Pat Riley
> Former coach
> of Los Angeles Lakers

A *vision* is a pictured goal.

Go For It!

The highest reward for man's toil is not what he gets for it but what he becomes by it.

— John Ruskin

Madeline Manning Mims was born in the ghetto in Cleveland, Ohio. An inner city child, she was told she would never be able to get out of her environment.

Everything was against her.

But she found that she could *run* out of the ghetto when she put God on the throne of her life.

She became an Olympic Gold and Silver Medalist, qualifying for the Olympics four consecutive times over sixteen years.

In 1921 in Harlem, New York, a small boy frequently was left with relatives so his parents could go on tour with their vaudeville troupes.

His mother was mean and abusive, often venting her temper on her young son. During his childhood, he stayed with many relatives who were alcoholics. He went to eighteen different schools before he graduated from high school.

At 13, he ran away on a bicycle, heading for California hunting an aunt who lived there. When his bicycle broke down, he stole rides on freight trains, eating whatever food other hoboes left behind.

Later, he served some time in the army, then began a radio career in the late 1940s. He went on to appear on other radio shows and then television programs.

Since then, he has written two poetry anthologies, two short-story collections, several novels, and other books.

He is an accomplished musician and noted as a lyricist, having written more than four thousand songs, including scores for Broadway plays.

In addition, he is a popular lecturer, and he wrote the PBS series, "The Meeting of the Minds," a historical dramatic presentation.

But perhaps Steve Allen is best known for creating the late-night talk show format for television. The talk show he created in 1953 went on the air in 1954 as "The Tonight Show"![9]

At some time, nearly everyone must live through a storm of some kind. Perhaps it is a "broken" heart, loss of a job, breakup of a marriage. Sooner or later, adversity comes to all of us.

That is the time when we wonder if life is worth living.

We wonder, "Is the dream worth the price?"

I say, "Yes! It is."

The time when many people throw up their hands in despair, give up, and quit is the best time to *go for it*.

We look at famous people, such as Steve Allen and Madeline Mims, and say, "They made it, and I could have too *if* I had their breaks, *if* I had been in their shoes."

We think the grass is greener in our neighbors' yard.

We use our hard times as excuses to justify lack of success.

We look enviously at the successes of others, whose lives seem so glamorous.

We say, "If times weren't so tough, I could get ahead."

However, if we could take everyone's problems and put them into a big pile, then pick the ones we wanted — more than likely, we would pick our own. If we look at other people's problems, not other people's successes, our own begin to take on a new perspective.

It has been my observation over the years that 90 percent of us bring our own defeats in various ways: by too much confidence or too little, by pessimism when things look good.

This is the time to *"go for it!"*

Winners Have No Sense of Blame

The one trait common to all great and consistent winners is the absence of an attitude of blame.

They do not pout or accuse when others are at fault.

They do not rage at themselves when they are at fault.

Occasionally, they may be beaten — but they never "beat" themselves.

Over the long haul, they win more often than they lose, frequently by allowing their opponents to beat themselves.

I am convinced temperament more than talent or brains determines whether a person is self-fulfilling or self-destroying.

The difference between one champion and another may be trifling in terms of durability, but vast in terms of heart.

You hear a great deal about the "killer instinct" in champions. All that means, I believe, is that in the ultimate showdown, a champion forgets himself and concentrates with passionate intensity upon his object.

The near-champion never forgets himself, never subordinates himself to the goal or the game.

I do not believe the winning determination is really an instinct to "kill" or to "conquer," but an instinct for perfection, a determination to complete something started, a perfection so exquisite in itself that it obliterates the man achieving it.

A winner is beyond praise and beyond blame. He, or she, does not "beat" himself or fight himself, *but forgets himself.*

It is time in your life to put aside blame, to assume responsibility and accountability, but to put your eyes and your efforts on the goal.

Go for it!

Sow Good Seeds

Resist the temptation to accept a job based on convenience or pressure from friends or family. Pour yourself into something in which you can believe.

Do not panic or talk doubt. Refuse to be intimidated by people or circumstances. But bold! Clothe courtesy with courage.

Do not mumble — look people in the eye when you speak. You are not a slave nor a "wimp."

Knowledge is power. The difference between failure and success is information.

There are two ways to learn:

• Experience (learning by our own mistakes), and

• Wisdom (learning from the mistakes of others).

Do not sell yourself short. Do not belittle yourself.

Spend time and attention on your personal growth and development. Invest in books, seminars, good clothing, and other things that will increase your confidence and sense of worth.

The better you treat yourself, the better you will be treated by others. Sow good seeds in the soil of your own life and mind.

The force, the mass of character, mind, heart, or soul that a man can put into any work, is the most important factor in that work.[10]

— A. P. Peabody

Be quick to listen.

In the insurance industry, it is said that million-dollar producers make statements while multi million-dollar producers ask questions.

Learn *how* to listen.

Listening is an art, an ability, and an incredible tool for personal growth.

Productive listening is vital for success.

Listening demands discipline, effort, and an unselfish attitude.

Listen to those around you, especially those who are hurting.

Listen to your own conscience, the key to real success.

Listen for the needs of others.

Listening also is "sowing good seeds."

A wise man will hear and will increase in learning.

— Proverbs 1:5

Even a fool, when he holdeth his peace, is counted wise, and he that shutteth his lips is esteemed a man of understanding.

— Proverbs 17:28

Surround Yourself With Good People

Invest time and seek the counsel of wise people. Be a student of those who succeeded before you. Appreciate the accomplishments of others.

Absorb the wisdom of others. Do not allow their personal shortcomings to dampen your enthusiasm. Take the best, and leave the rest. Value the counsel of the learned.

He that walketh with wise men shall be wise.

— Proverbs 13:20

In a multitude of counselors there is safety.

— Proverbs 11:4

Relationships are important to success.

The most important relationship a man ever will have is with God. Spending time with God, reading his Word, communicating with Him through prayer, and letting Him communicate with you, is the best way to be victorious.

Next in importance comes your relationship with your spouse.

Third in impact upon your life are the people you choose to surround yourself with. They can make all the difference in the world.

Paul Harvey once said to me, "Van, if you want to get big fleas, hang out with big dogs!"

You should be careful who is allowed in your inner circle of friends. I do not mean to be "stand-offish," aloof, or elitist. However, you do need to make sure that the people with whom you associate the most often are in agreement with you and encourage you to move to a higher level.

Your closest friends should be people you respect, people who are diligent and conscientious. You not only will have more fun in life, but you will reach your goals quicker.

One of the most exciting things I found in the insurance industry was the "push" I got from belonging to a study group. Most of the people in the group were more advanced in the business than I was. They had more years of experience and were doing more business.

Because of the synergistic effect of the group's coming together, sharing ideas, keeping track of each other and where everyone was in production, pulled each of us up to a level where, as individuals, we would not have reached until many years later.

And the way to become truly useful is to seek the best that other brains have to offer. Use them to supplement your own, and give credit to them when they have helped.[11]

— Gordon Dean

A relationship group is not meant to be a means of letting other people do your thinking for you. Far from it! Such a group is meant to stimulate your own thinking through the association with other minds.

No one person can know everything. The more sympathetic minds — by "sympathetic," I mean those working for a common purpose — the more related information is going to be available. Great ideas usually result from a combination of related information.

You can also "surround yourself" with wise people through books, tapes, and videos.

All that mankind has done, thought, or been is lying as in magic preservation in the pages of books.[12]

— Carlyle

Winning Attitudes

Be willing to grow into greatness.

As a small acorn grows into a great oak tree, so grow the seeds of greatness within our lives:

It takes work and discipline.

It takes proper nurturing.

It takes time and may not happen overnight.

Resist impatience. As you assume responsibility for the present, take time to enjoy the things available to you right now.

Constantly hold before you the dream toward which you work.

Happiness is feeling good about yourself, and that depends very much on your productivity.

Productivity depends on your ability to set up a list of daily tasks in order of importance and accomplish them.

Avoid a complaining attitude.

Speak with enthusiasm and authority. None of us ever gets a second chance to make a first impression. Project the impression of a winner. The way you talk, dress, and act reveals much about your character. Dress neatly. Avoid the sloppiness which suggests a careless lifestyle.

A winner never condescends but lifts others around him to a higher level of encouragement. Help others attain their success, and you will help yourself.

Go for it!

Build a climate of confidence.

Information breeds confidence. Know *what* you believe and *why* you believe it. Disconnect the memory of past failures. Stop advertising your mistakes. Remind yourself of good decisions and triumphs of the past. See yourself winning.

Manage your time.

As I said earlier, control your time, and manage it wisely. Why? Because time is money. Treat time with the wisdom it deserves. Determine what you want to accomplish each day, each week, or each month, and set deadlines for the attainment of these goals.

Avoid time wasters — bored friends, unnecessary phone calls, idle chatter.

A day that is a social success usually is a business failure.

Be merciful.

What you make happen for others, God will make happen for you.

What you sow today determines your harvest tomorrow. Sow kindness; be slow to criticize and quick to forgive. Love produces a nonjudgmental climate that will also affect you.

Become a part of someone's miracle, and it will come back to you.

Give favor and expect to receive favor. Expect others to respond favorably toward you.

Do not build mental "monsters" of fear and worry.

If a salesman expects rejection, he will multiply the possibilities and usually receive it.

Plan now for financial freedom.

Success does not "just happen." You set it in motion.

So it is with financial freedom.

You will never change where you are until you change what you are doing.

Live within your means. Do not let your upkeep be your downfall. Live with the means presently provided, and budget to correct improper and harmful spending habits.

Work hard, and be diligent, but respect your body.

Do not succumb to the "furniture disease";

That is when your chest falls into your drawers.

Health is life's first prize. Men spend their health getting wealth, then gladly pay all they have gained to get their health back!

Be good to your body. Give it sleep and proper nutrition. Exercise it, and give it the surroundings it needs. Your body is the only "machine" God will allow you during your lifetime. Value it, and take care of it.

Learn how to talk rightly, and tame your tongue.

The most powerful force in your life is your tongue. Proverbs 18:21 says, "Death and life are in the power of the tongue."

Your tongue can destroy or build, tear up or mend.

Use your words to build confidence in others. Refuse to gossip about or slander anyone else. Learn to keep confidences. To control your tongue is to control your very life.

Learn how to handle criticism.

When you decide to *go for it*, you probably will receive some.

The human heart craves acceptance and approval; rejection destroys our motivation. However, criticism can be productive or destructive, depending on how you receive it. Analyze the source, the purpose, and the solution.

Do not give any more time to a critic than you would to a friend; but, being teachable is one sign of a true winner.

Be honest.

The power of an honest life is remarkable. Integrity cannot be purchased.

There re two forces that build the gigantic machine called credibility which opens the door to success: trustworthiness and expertise.

Honesty is the hinge that swings the golden door of prosperity and success.

Never, never, never give up.

Winners are just ex-losers who got mad. The battle belongs to the persistent. The victory will go to the one who does not quit. Refuse to let friends or circumstances defeat you.

If you have been defeated, remember that from the ashes of defeat burn the greatest fires of accomplishment. Your past is the fertilizer for the future, as I said before.

God made you to climb and not crawl.

God made you to fly and not fall.

God made you to swim and not sink.

You were not made to dig in the dirt with the chickens, but to soar in the clouds with the wings of an eagle.

Go for it!

Today is *your* day.

Endnotes

[1]This entire chapter is adapted from *Stay in the Game — It's Too Soon To Quit* by Van Crouch, (Tulsa: Honor Books, 1989) pp. 13-22, 189-207.

[2]Campbell, Dr. David. *If you Don't Know Where You're Going, You Will Probably Wind Up Somewhere Else* (Argus Communications, 1974).

[3]Waitley, Denis. *The Joy of Working*, (New York: Dodd, Mead & Company. Copyright © 1985 by Larimi Communications Associates, Inc.), p. 43.

[4]Ziglar, Zig. *See You at the Top*, (Dallas: Pelican Publishing Company. Copyright © 1975 by Zig Ziglar), p. 149. Used by permission of the Pelican Publishing Co.

[5]Waitley. *Joy*, p. 39.

[6]Tan, Paul Lee. *Encyclopedia of 7700 Illustrations* (Maryland: Rockville, Assurance Publishers. Copyright © 1979 by Paul Lee Tan, ninth printing), p. 1566, Epigram.

[7]Ziglar. *See You*, p. 148.

[8]Jones, Charles. *Life Is Tremendous* (Wheaton: Tyndale House Publishers. Copyright © 1981).

[9]DeMaris, Ovid. "The Other Side of Laughter; the Pain the Gain, the Life of Steve Allen," *Parade Magazine*, pp. 4-9. Reprinted with permission from *Parade*, Copyright © May 5, 1985.

[10]*The New Dictionary*, p. 741.

[11]Quote from the late Gordon Dean, former chairman of the Atomic Energy Commission. Taken from *Sourcebook of 500 Illustrations* by Robert G. Lee, p. 100. Copyright © 1964 by Zondervan Publishing House. Used by permission.

[12]Tan. *Encyclopedia of Illustrations*, p. 215, #550.

3

PLANNING YOUR LIFE TO BE A WINNER

by

R. Henry Migliore

1. The difference between the winner of the PGA Golf Tournament and the tenth player is an average of one stroke, the fiftieth player only four strokes. You have to be a really good golfer to even be in the top 200, but a margin of only six strokes separates the top from the 200th player.

2. In a study of aerodynamics, one learns that the leading portion of the wing provides most of an airplane's lift. Of all the square feet of space in the plane, only this very small area up and down each wing provides the margin to lift the plane.

3. The launching of the Columbia spaceship was an intricate maneuver. Everything had to be exact in terms of the centrifugal force of the earth's movement, the launching speed, and the power as the spaceship was thrust into space. The slightest margin of error on the launch would have caused the spaceship to be off hundreds of thousands of miles as it went into orbit.

4. Everyone enjoyed the NCAA basketball championship playoff a few years ago between Georgetown and North Carolina. They played shot-for-shot and point-for-point for forty minutes. With fifteen seconds to go and Georgetown behind by one point, the final play of the game was the margin of difference between being the NCAA champion and finishing in second place.

5. If you study a football game, you will find that five or six key plays make the difference in the game. If the coaches knew which plays these would be, they would practice all week on those particular plays to be sure they are executed with perfection. The problem is that out of the eighty to one hundred plays executed, one does not know which are the key plays. This forces players to execute with precision on all of the plays so that the six or seven are executed properly. The margin for winning boils down to a very few plays.

6. The difference between winning and losing in our lives can be measured by the margin. Whenever the marginal play comes along, you will excel, and in the process, become all that you can be.

7. As much as we want to think of something as glamorous and fascinating, there is always a gritty side we have not seen. The most precious gem was once buried in dirt — and to be truly beautiful — it must be polished and cut and set

in the right light. In its original state it was just as worthy, but its full potential was not known until someone recognized it and was willing and patient enough to set it free. The right amount of polishing is needed so you can realize your potential. It is not necessarily what we can see on the outside that makes anyone or anything beautiful. It is that glow from the inside. There is always work to be done, a need to keep on refining, polishing, and simplifying. Every person has the opportunity to receive that inner glow, to be refined and polished. All we have to do is accept Jesus as our personal Savior. He provides the margin we need as we make our walk through life.

8. We owe it to ourselves to bring out the best of who we are — to use our talents for something beautiful — and worthy. That requires a staying power that comes only with vision and determination.

9. You need a plan to become what the Lord wants you to be. Here are the essential steps: a) have a vision/dream, b) get the facts, be aware of what is going on around you, c) analyze your strengths and weaknesses, d) make a few assumptions, e) set definite measurable objectives, f) be in a state of continual prayer (God will confirm, through the Holy Spirit, what is right for you), g) develop a list of strategies for each objective, h) put the plan into action, i) review progress, and j) reward yourself for accomplishment.

"Point of View"

Twenty Sure Ways To Lose Money[2]

After twenty years of helping people solve business and personal problems, I have discovered a few ways to lose one's hard-earned money. Listen carefully for these phrases, and your objective will soon be attained:

— This opportunity is available for only a short time. . .

— You have been selected as a winner of a fabulous prize. You must. . .

— All your friends are in on this. . .

— You have earned the right, through your success, to be considered for. . .

—I am a (Christian, member of a lodge or club, and so forth). Do business with me. . .

Keep talking to the person who has this opening line and soon he will have, as the popular country song says, "the gold mine, and you will have the shaft."

Here are some rules to consider if your aim is to lose your money quickly:

1. Let someone else, preferably someone you do not know, bring you the investment idea. If they come to your door, by all means, let them in.

2. Constantly worry and plot against paying taxes. Find ways to lose so that you can deduct the losses from your taxes.

3. Buy expensive advertising in the yellow pages instead of finding the most effective and financially efficient form of advertising for you.

4. Be arrogant and have a "godlike" air.

5. Try to get rich quickly.

6. For the ultimate experience, invest money you cannot afford to lose.

7. Respond quickly with action when your mate says, "Why don't you do as well as _____?"

8. Give your mate and children credit cards and no budget.

9. Send your children to college with no accountability. Provide a car, if possible. Keep them in college no matter what.

10. Use the phone and save those letters, postcards, and stamps.

11. Buy raw land, the farther away from home, the better.

12. Build your wife a bigger closet.

13. Go into a business you know nothing about to spend extra money trying to find out how to run it.

14. Do not develop a personal life plan, a financial plan, or set goals.

15. Do not buy insurance of any kind.

16. Do not make out your own personal will. Watch your loved ones from Heaven while

they fight over your estate and give most of it to lawyers.

17. Get a divorce.

18. Do a lot of impulse buying.

19. Keep all your money for yourself. Do not give to your church or any worthy cause.

20. Do not ask for any advice from professionals in banking, insurance, law, investments, and accounting.

This information is meant to make all of us think before we spend. We all have most likely made some poor economic decisions and learned good lessons. Our quality of life can be affected by our economic decisions. It is to be hoped that we will be more careful and think through how we invest and spend our money.

Endnote

'This entire chapter is from *Personal Action Planning, How to Know What You Want and Get It* (Tulsa: Honor Books, 1988) pp. 69-71, 95-97

Part II
Wisdom Through the
Scripture

4

DEVELOPING YOUR RELATIONSHIP WITH GOD

Jesus, Your Savior

Just as Moses lifted up the snake in the desert, so the Son of Man must be lifted up,

That everyone who believes in him may have eternal life.

For God so loved the world that he gave his one and only Son, that whoever believes in him shall not perish but have eternal life.

For God did not send his Son into the world to condemn the world, but to save the world through him.

Whoever believes in him is not condemned, but whoever does not believe stands condemned already because he has not believed in the name of God's one and only Son.

John 3:14-18

For my Father's will is that everyone who looks to the Son and believes in him shall have eternal life, and I will raise him up at the last day.

John 6:40

In reply Jesus declared, "I tell you the truth, no one can see the kingdom of God unless he is born again."

John 3:3

I tell you the truth, he who believes has everlasting life.

I am the bread of life.

John 6:47,48

For just as the Father raises the dead and gives them life, even so the Son gives life to whom he is pleased to give it.

Moreover, the Father judges no one, but has entrusted all judgment to the Son,

That all may honor the Son just as they honor the Father. He who does not honor the Son does not honor the Father, who sent him.

I tell you the truth, whoever hears my word and believes him who sent me has eternal life and will not be condemned; he has crossed over from death to life.

I tell you the truth, a time is coming and has now come when the dead will hear the voice of the Son of God and those who hear will live.

For as the Father has life in himself, so he has granted the Son to have life in himself.

John 5:21-26

But he continued, "You are from below; I am from above. You are of this world; I am not of this world.

"I told you that you would die in your sins; if you do not believe that I am [the one I claim to be], you will indeed die in your sins."

John 8:23,24

The Father loves the Son and has placed everything in his hands.

Whoever believes in the Son has eternal life, but whoever rejects the Son will not see life, for God's wrath remains on him.

John 3:35,36

The thief comes only to steal and kill and destroy; I have come that they may have life, and have it to the full.

John 10:10

For there is one God and one mediator between God and men, the man Christ Jesus,

Who gave himself as a ransom for all men — the testimony given in its proper time.

1 Timothy 2:5,6

Then Jesus cried out, "When a man believes in me, he does not believe in me only, but in the one who sent me.

"When he looks at me, he sees the one who sent me.

"I have come into the world as a light, so that no one who believes in me should stay in darkness."

John 12:44-46

My sheep listen to my voice; I know them, and they follow me.

I give them eternal life, and they shall never perish; no one can snatch them out of my hand.

My Father, who has given them to me, is greater than all; no one can snatch them out of my Father's hand.

I and the Father are one.

John 10:27-30

Jesus said to her, "I am the resurrection and the life. He who believes in me will live, even though he dies;

"And whoever lives and believes in me will never die. Do you believe this?"

John 11:25,26

Jesus answered, "I am the way and the truth and the life. No one comes to the Father except through me."

John 14:6

And everyone who calls on the name of the Lord will be saved.

Acts 2:21

Peter replied, "Repent and be baptized, every one of you, in the name of Jesus Christ for the forgiveness of your sins. And you will receive the gift of the Holy Spirit."

Acts 2:38

Repent, then, and turn to God, so that your sins may be wiped out, that times of refreshing may come from the Lord.

Acts 3:19

Then know this, you and all the people of Israel: It is by the name of Jesus Christ of Nazareth, whom you crucified but whom God raised from the dead, that this man stands before you healed.

He is "'the stone you builders rejected, which has become the capstone.'

"Salvation is found in no one else, for there is no other name under heaven given to men by which we must be saved."

Acts 4:10-12

No! We believe it is through the grace of our Lord Jesus that we are saved, just as they are.

Acts 15:11

For it is by grace you have been saved, through faith — and this not from yourselves, it is the gift of God —

Not by works, so that no one can boast.

Ephesians 2:8,9

That if you confess with your mouth, "Jesus is Lord," and believe in your heart that God raised him from the dead, you will be saved.

For it is with your heart that you believe and are justified, and it is with your mouth that you confess and are saved.

Romans 10:9,10

For Christ died for sins once for all, the righteous for the unrighteous, to bring you to God. He was put to death in the body but made alive by the Spirit.

1 Peter 3:18

Yet to all who received him, to those who believed in his name, he gave the right to become children of God —

Children born not of natural descent, nor of human decision or a husband's will, but born of God.

John 1:12,13

Examples of God's Character in the Bible

The Lord is my strength and my shield; my heart trusts in him, and I am helped. My heart leaps for joy and I will give thanks to him in song.

Psalm 28:7

Taste and see that the Lord is good; blessed is the man who takes refuge in him.

Psalm 34:8

Who among the gods is like you, O Lord? Who is like you — majestic in holiness, awesome in glory, working wonders?

You stretched out your right hand and the earth swallowed them.

In your unfailing love you will lead the people you have redeemed. In your strength you will guide them to your holy dwelling.

Exodus 15:11-13

The Lord is my light and my salvation — whom shall I fear? The Lord is the stronghold of my life — of whom shall I be afraid?

Psalm 27:1

The Lord is my strength and my song; he has become my salvation. He is my God, and I will praise him, my father's God, and I will exalt him.

The Lord is a warrior; the Lord is his name.

Exodus 15:2,3

Then the Lord came down in the cloud and stood there with him and proclaimed his name, the Lord.

And he passed in front of Moses, proclaiming, "The Lord, the Lord, the compassionate and gracious God, slow to anger, abounding in love and faithfulness,

Maintaining love to thousands, and forgiving wickedness, rebellion and sin. Yet he does not leave the guilty unpunished; he punishes the children and their children for the sin of the fathers to the third and fourth generation."

Exodus 34:5-7

The Lord is a refuge for the oppressed, a stronghold in times of trouble.

Those who know your name will trust in you, for you, Lord, have never forsaken those who seek you.

Psalm 9:9,10

I love you, O Lord, my strength.

The Lord is my rock, my fortress and my deliverer; my God is my rock, in whom I take refuge. He is my shield and the horn of my salvation, my stronghold.

I call to the Lord, who is worthy of praise, and I am saved from my enemies.

Psalm 18:1-3

How great is your goodness, which you have stored up for those who fear you, which you bestow in the sight of men on those who take refuge in you.

In the shelter of your presence you hide them from the intrigues of men; in your dwelling you keep them safe from accusing tongues.

Psalm 31:19,20

You are my hiding place; you will protect me from trouble and surround me with songs of deliverance. *Selah*

Psalm 32:7

But the eyes of the Lord are on those who fear him, on those whose hope is in his unfailing love,

To deliver them from death and keep them alive in famine.

We wait in hope for the Lord; he is our help and our shield.

In him our hearts rejoice, for we trust in his holy name.

May your unfailing love rest upon us, O Lord, even as we put our hope in you.

Psalm 33:18-22

And they were calling to one another: "Holy, holy, holy is the Lord Almighty; the whole earth is full of his glory."

Isaiah 6:3

Keep your lives free from the love of money and be content with what you have, because God has said, "Never will I leave you; never will I forsake you."

So we say with confidence, "The Lord is my helper; I will not be afraid. What can man do to me?"

Hebrews 13:5,6

God, who has called you into fellowship with his Son Jesus Christ our Lord, is faithful.

1 Corinthians 1:9

The righteous cry out, and the Lord hears them; he delivers them from all their troubles.

The Lord is close to the brokenhearted and saves those who are crushed in spirit.

Psalm 34:17,18

The salvation of the righteous comes from the Lord; he is their stronghold in time of trouble.

The Lord helps them and delivers them; he delivers them from the wicked and saves them, because they take refuge in him.

Psalm 37:39,40

Blessed are those you choose and bring near to live in your courts! We are filled with the good things of your house, of your holy temple.

Psalm 65:4

As a father has compassion on his children, so the Lord has compassion on those who fear him;

For he knows how we are formed, he remembers that we are dust.

Psalm 103:13,14

For the Lord God is a sun and shield; the Lord bestows favor and honor; no good thing does he withhold from those whose walk is blameless.

O Lord Almighty, blessed is the man who trusts in you.

Psalm 84:11,12

He who dwells in the shelter of the Most High will rest in the shadow of the Almighty.

I will say of the Lord, "He is my refuge and my fortress, my God, in whom I trust."

Surely he will save you from the fowler's snare and from the deadly pestilence.

He will cover you with his feathers, and under his wings you will find refuge; his faithfulness will be your shield and rampart.

Psalm 91:1-4

Great are the works of the Lord; they are pondered by all who delight in them.

Glorious and majestic are his deeds, and his righteousness endures forever.

He has caused his wonders to be remembered; the Lord is gracious and compassionate.

He provides food for those who fear him; he remembers his covenant forever.

He has shown his people the power of his works, giving them the lands of other nations.

The works of his hands are faithful and just; all his precepts are trustworthy.

They are steadfast for ever and ever, done in faithfulness and uprightness.

He provided redemption for his people; he ordained his covenant forever — holy and awesome is his name.

Psalm 111:2-9

We proclaim to you what we have seen and heard, so that you also may have fellowship with us. And our fellowship is with the Father and with his Son, Jesus Christ.

We write this to make our joy complete.

1 John 1:3,4

But if we walk in the light, as he is in the light, we have fellowship with one another, and the blood of Jesus, his Son, purifies us from all sin.

1 John 1:7

The Lord is with me; I will not be afraid. What can man do to me?

Psalm 118:6

But Zion said, "The Lord has forsaken me, the Lord has forgotten me."

"Can a mother forget the baby at her breast and have no compassion on the child she has borne? Though she may forget, I will not forget you!

"See, I have engraved you on the palms of my hands; your walls are ever before me."

Isaiah 49:14-16

For this is what the high and lofty One says — he who lives forever, whose name is holy: "I live in a high and holy place, but also with him who is contrite and lowly in spirit, to revive the spirit of the lowly and to revive the heart of the contrite."

Isaiah 57:15

Do you not know that he who unites himself with a prostitute is one with her in body? For it is said, "The two will become one flesh."

But he who unites himself with the Lord is one with him in spirit.

Flee from sexual immorality. All other sins a man commits are outside his body, but he who sins sexually sins against his own body.

1 Corinthians 6:16-18

This is the covenant I will make with the house of Israel after that time, declares the Lord. I will put my laws in their minds and write them on their hearts. I will be their God, and they will be my people.

No longer will a man teach his neighbor, or a man his brother, saying, "Know the Lord," because they will all know me, from the least of them to the greatest.

Hebrews 8:10,11

And the scripture was fulfilled that says, "Abraham believed God, and it was credited to him as righteousness," and he was called God's friend.

James 2:23

I will walk among you and be your God, and you will be my people.

Leviticus 26:12

The Lord is not slow in keeping his promise, as some understand slowness. He is patient with you, not wanting anyone to perish, but everyone to come to repentance.

2 Peter 3:9

Who wants all men to be saved and to come to a knowledge of the truth.

1 Timothy 2:4

Sharing With God in Prayer

This is the confidence we have in approaching God: that if we ask anything according to his will, he hears us.

And if we know that he hears us — whatever we ask — we know that we have what we asked of him.

1 John 5:14,15

Come and listen, all you who fear God; let me tell you what he has done for me.

I cried out to him with my mouth; his praise was on my tongue.

If I had cherished sin in my heart, the Lord would not have listened;

But God has surely listened and heard my voice in prayer.

Praise be to God, who has not rejected my prayer or withheld his love from me!

Psalm 66:16-20

I, even I, am he who blots out your transgressions, for my own sake, and remembers your sins no more.

Review the past for me, let us argue the matter together; state the case for your innocence.

Isaiah 43:25,26

We proclaim to you what we have seen and heard, so that you also may have fellowship with us. And our fellowship is with the Father and with his Son, Jesus Christ.

1 John 1:3

I sought the Lord, and he answered me; he delivered me from all my fears.

Those who look to him are radiant; their faces are never covered with shame.

This poor man called, and the Lord heard him; he saved him out of all his troubles.

The angel of the Lord encamps around those who fear him, and he delivers them.

Psalm 34:4-7

Seeking God's Face With Your Whole Heart

Trust in him at all times, O people; pour out your hearts to him, for God is our refuge. *Selah*

Psalm 62:8

One thing I ask of the Lord, this is what I seek: that I may dwell in the house of the Lord all the days of my life, to gaze upon the beauty of the Lord and to seek him in his temple.

Psalm 27:4

My heart says of you, "Seek his face!" Your face, Lord, I will seek.

Do not hide your face from me, do not turn your servant away in anger; you have been my helper. Do not reject me or forsake me, O God my Savior.

Psalm 27:8,9

Fear the Lord, you his saints, for those who fear him lack nothing.

The lions may grow weak and hungry, but those who seek the Lord lack no good thing.

Psalm 34:9,10

As the deer pants for streams of water, so my soul pants for you, O God.

My soul thirsts for God, for the living God. When can I go and meet with God?

Psalm 42:1,2

O God, you are my God, earnestly I seek you; my soul thirsts for you, my body longs for you, in a dry and weary land where there is no water.

I have seen you in the sanctuary and beheld your power and your glory.

Because your love is better than life, my lips will glorify you.

I will praise you as long as I live, and in your name I will lift up my hands.

Psalm 63:1-4

The poor will see and be glad — you who seek God, may your hearts live!

Psalm 69:32

Yet I am always with you; you hold me by my right hand.

You guide me with your counsel, and afterward you will take me into glory.

Whom have I in heaven but you? And earth has nothing I desire besides you.

My flesh and my heart may fail, but God is the strength of my heart and my portion forever.

Those who are far from you will perish; you destroy all who are unfaithful to you.

But as for me, it is good to be near God. I have made the Sovereign Lord my refuge; I will tell of all your deeds.

Psalm 73:23-28

My soul yearns, even faints, for the courts of the Lord; my heart and my flesh cry out for the living God.

Psalm 84:2

The Lord looks down from heaven on the sons of men to see if there are any who understand, any who seek God.

Psalm 14:2

Such is the generation of those who seek him, who seek your face, O God of Jacob. *Selah*

Psalm 24:6

Glory in his holy name; let the hearts of those who seek the Lord rejoice.

Look to the Lord and his strength; seek his face always.

Psalm 105:3,4

Yes, Lord, walking in the way of your laws, we wait for you; your name and renown are the desire of our hearts.

My soul yearns for you in the night; in the morning my spirit longs for you. When your judgments come upon the earth, the people of the world learn righteousness.

Isaiah 26:8,9

But whatever was to my profit I now consider loss for the sake of Christ.

What is more, I consider everything a loss compared to the surpassing greatness of knowing Christ Jesus my Lord, for whose sake I have lost all things. I consider them rubbish, that I may gain Christ

And be found in him, not having a righteousness of my own that comes from the

law, but that which is through faith in Christ —
the righteousness that comes from God and is by
faith.

I want to know Christ and the power of
his resurrection and the fellowship of sharing
in his sufferings, becoming like him in his
death,

And so, somehow, to attain to the
resurrection from the dead.

Not that I have already obtained all this, or
have already been made perfect, but I press on to
take hold of that for which Christ Jesus took hold
of me.

Philippians 3:7-12

Come near to God and he will come near to
you. Wash your hands, you sinners, and purify
your hearts, you double-minded.

James 4:8

I seek you with all my heart; do not let me
stray from your commands.

Psalm 119:10

Love the Lord your God with all your heart
and with all your soul and with all your
strength.

Deuteronomy 6:5

So be very careful to love the Lord your God.

Joshua 23:11

Loving God Through Praise and Worship

Rejoice in the Lord always. I will say it again: Rejoice!

Philippians 4:4

He who sacrifices thank offerings honors me, and he prepares the way so that I may show him the salvation of God.

Psalm 50:23

Be exalted, O Lord, in your strength; we will sing and praise your might.

Psalm 21:13

Sing joyfully to the Lord, you righteous; it is fitting for the upright to praise him.

Praise the Lord with the harp; make music to him on the ten-stringed lyre.

Sing to him a new song; play skillfully, and shout for joy.

Psalm 33:1-3

Let them give thanks to the Lord for his unfailing love and his wonderful deeds for men,

For he satisfies the thirsty and fills the hungry with good things.

Psalm 107:8,9

Offer right sacrifices and trust in the Lord.

Psalm 4:5

I will praise you, O Lord, with all my heart; I will tell of all your wonders.

I will be glad and rejoice in you; I will sing praise to your name, O Most High.

Psalm 9:1,2

Love the Lord, all his saints! The Lord preserves the faithful, but the proud he pays back in full.

Be strong and take heart, all you who hope in the Lord.

Psalm 31:23,24

I will extol the Lord at all times; his praise will always be on my lips.

My soul will boast in the Lord; let the afflicted hear and rejoice.

Glorify the Lord with me; let us exalt his name together.

Psalm 34:1-3

Come, let us sing for joy to the Lord; let us shout aloud to the Rock of our salvation.

Let us come before him with thanksgiving and extol him with music and song.

For the Lord is the great God, the great King above all gods.

Psalm 95:1-3

If you love me, you will obey what I command.

John 14:15

"Shout and be glad, O Daughter of Zion. For I am coming, and I will live among you," declares the Lord.

Zechariah 2:10

5

YOUR RELATIONSHIPS

Conflict at Home in Your Family

Blessed are the peacemakers, for they will be called sons of God.

Matthew 5:9

Do not judge, and you will not be judged. Do not condemn, and you will not be condemned. Forgive, and you will be forgiven.

Luke 6:37

My dear brothers, take note of this: Everyone should be quick to listen, slow to speak and slow to become angry,

For man's anger does not bring about the righteous life that God desires.

James 1:19,20

"In your anger do not sin": Do not let the sun go down while you are still angry,

And do not give the devil a foothold.

He who has been stealing must steal no longer, but must work, doing something useful with his own hands, that he may have something to share with those in need.

Do not let any unwholesome talk come out of your mouths, but only what is helpful for building others up according to their needs, that it may benefit those who listen.

And do not grieve the Holy Spirit of God, with whom you were sealed for the day of redemption.

Get rid of all bitterness, rage and anger, brawling and slander, along with every form of malice.

Be kind and compassionate to one another, forgiving each other, just as in Christ God forgave you.

Ephesians 4:26-32

But if you harbor bitter envy and selfish ambition in your hearts, do not boast about it or deny the truth.

Such "wisdom" does not come down from heaven but is earthly, unspiritual, of the devil.

For where you have envy and selfish ambition, there you find disorder and every evil practice.

But the wisdom that comes from heaven is first of all pure; then peace-loving, considerate, submissive, full of mercy and good fruit, impartial and sincere.

Peacemakers who sow in peace raise a harvest of righteousness.

James 3:14-18

A gentle answer turns away wrath, but a harsh word stirs up anger.

The tongue of the wise commends knowledge, but the mouth of the fool gushes folly.

The eyes of the Lord are everywhere, keeping watch on the wicked and the good.

The tongue that brings healing is a tree of life, but a deceitful tongue crushes the spirit.

Proverbs 15:1-4

Therefore, as God's chosen people, holy and dearly loved, clothe yourselves with compassion, kindness, humility, gentleness and patience.

Bear with each other and forgive whatever grievances you may have against one another. Forgive as the Lord forgave you.

And over all these virtues put on love, which binds them all together in perfect unity.

Colossians 3:12-14

Hatred stirs up dissension, but love covers over all wrongs.

Proverbs 10:12

Finding Godly Friends

He who walks with the wise grows wise, but a companion of fools suffers harm.

Proverbs 13:20

A friend loves at all times, and a brother is born for adversity.

Proverbs 17:17

Do two walk together unless they have agreed to do so?

Amos 3:3

You adulterous people, don't you know that friendship with the world is hatred toward God? Anyone who chooses to be a friend of the world becomes an enemy of God.

James 4:4

He who keeps the law is a discerning son, but a companion of gluttons disgraces his father.

Proverbs 28:7

Stay away from a foolish man, for you will not find knowledge on his lips.

Proverbs 14:7

Do not make friends with a hot-tempered man, do not associate with one easily angered,

Or you may learn his ways and get yourself ensnared.

Proverbs 22:24,25

Your rulers are rebels, companions of thieves; they all love bribes and chase after gifts. They do not defend the cause of the fatherless; the widow's case does not come before them.

Isaiah 1:23

Sometimes you were publicly exposed to insult and persecution; at other times you stood side by side with those who were so treated.

Hebrews 10:33

A man of many companions may come to ruin, but there is a friend who sticks closer than a brother.

Proverbs 18:24

Perfume and incense bring joy to the heart, and the pleasantness of one's friend springs from his earnest counsel.

Proverbs 27:9

Flee the evil desires of youth, and pursue righteousness, faith, love and peace, along with those who call on the Lord out of a pure heart.

2 Timothy 2:22

Blessed is the man who does not walk in the counsel of the wicked or stand in the way of sinners or sit in the seat of mockers.

But his delight is in the law of the Lord, and on his law he meditates day and night.

He is like a tree planted by streams of water, which yields its fruit in season and whose leaf does not wither. Whatever he does prospers.

Psalm 1:1-3

I am a friend to all who fear you, to all who follow your precepts.

Psalm 119:63

Thus you will walk in the ways of good men and keep to the paths of the righteous.

Proverbs 2:20

With whom I once enjoyed sweet fellowship as we walked with the throng at the house of God.

Psalm 55:14

6

BIBLE PROMISES IN TIMES OF NEED

Bible Promises for Gaining Ability

I can do everything through him who gives me strength.

Philippians 4:13

I always thank God for you because of his grace given you in Christ Jesus.

For in him you have been enriched in every way — in all your speaking and in all your knowledge —

Because our testimony about Christ was confirmed in you.

Therefore you do not lack any spiritual gift as you eagerly wait for our Lord Jesus Christ to be revealed.

1 Corinthians 1:4-7

And I have filled him with the Spirit of God, with skill, ability and knowledge in all kinds of crafts.

Exodus 31:3

If you remain in me and my words remain in you, ask whatever you wish, and it will be given you.

John 15:7

Each one should use whatever gift he has received to serve others, faithfully administering God's grace in its various forms.

If anyone speaks, he should do it as one speaking the very words of God. If anyone serves, he should do it with the strength God provides, so that in all things God may be praised through Jesus Christ. To him be the glory and the power for ever and ever. Amen.

1 Peter 4:10,11

Moreover, I have appointed Oholiab son of Ahisamach, of the tribe of Dan, to help him. Also I have given skill to all the craftsmen to make everything I have commanded you.

Exodus 31:6

Who have been chosen according to the foreknowledge of God the Father, through the sanctifying work of the Spirit, for obedience to Jesus Christ and sprinkling by his blood: Grace and peace be yours in abundance.

His divine power has given us everything we need for life and godliness through our knowledge of him who called us by his own glory and goodness.

2 Peter 1:2,3

Praise be to the Lord my Rock, who trains my hands for war, my fingers for battle.

Psalm 144:1

Remain in me, and I will remain in you. No branch can bear fruit by itself; it must remain in the vine. Neither can you bear fruit unless you remain in me.

I am the vine; you are the branches. If a man remains in me and I in him, he will bear much fruit; apart from me you can do nothing.

John 15:4,5

With your help I can advance against a troop; with my God I can scale a wall.

Psalm 18:29

No, in all these things we are more than conquerors through him who loved us.

Romans 8:37

And my God will meet all your needs according to his glorious riches in Christ Jesus.

Philippians 4:19

Bible Promises for Finding Friends

Delight yourself in the Lord and he will give you the desires of your heart.

Psalm 37:4

A man of many companions may come to ruin, but there is a friend who sticks closer than a brother.

Proverbs 18:24

A friend loves at all times, and a brother is born for adversity.

Proverbs 17:17

He who walks with the wise grows wise, but a companion of fools suffers harm.

Proverbs 13:20

Do nothing out of selfish ambition or vain conceit, but in humility consider others better than yourselves.

Each of you should look not only to your own interests, but also to the interests of others.

Philippians 2:3,4

For the Lord God is a sun and shield; the Lord bestows favor and honor; no good thing does he withhold from those whose walk is blameless.

Psalm 84:11

Bible Promises for Being Comforted

And I will ask the Father, and he will give you another Counselor to be with you forever —

The Spirit of truth. The world cannot accept him, because it neither sees him nor knows him. But you know him, for he lives with you and will be in you.

I will not leave you as orphans; I will come to you.

John 14:16-18

But I tell you the truth: It is for your good that I am going away. Unless I go away, the Counselor will not come to you; but if I go, I will send him to you.

John 16:7

But the Counselor, the Holy Spirit, whom the Father will send in my name, will teach you all things and will remind you of everything I have said to you.

John 14:26

Therefore encourage one another and build each other up, just as in fact you are doing.

1 Thessalonians 5:11

Praise be to the God and Father of our Lord Jesus Christ, the Father of compassion and the God of all comfort,

Who comforts us in all our troubles, so that we can comfort those in any trouble with the comfort we ourselves have received from God.

For just as the sufferings of Christ flow over into our lives, so also through Christ our comfort overflows.

2 Corinthians 1:3-5

David was greatly distressed because the men were talking of stoning him; each one was bitter in spirit because of his sons and daughters. But David found strength in the Lord his God.

1 Samuel 30:6

The eternal God is your refuge, and underneath are the everlasting arms. He will drive out your enemy before you, saying, "Destroy him!"

Deuteronomy 33:27

Even though I walk through the valley of the shadow of death, I will fear no evil, for you are with me; your rod and your staff, they comfort me.

Psalm 23:4

For in the day of trouble he will keep me safe in his dwelling; he will hide me in the shelter of his tabernacle and set me high upon a rock.

Then my head will be exalted above the enemies who surround me; at his tabernacle will I sacrifice with shouts of joy; I will sing and make music to the Lord.

Psalm 27:5,6

For his anger lasts only a moment, but his favor lasts a lifetime; weeping may remain for a night, but rejoicing comes in the morning.

Psalm 30:5

I will be glad and rejoice in your love, for you saw my affliction and knew the anguish of my soul.

Psalm 31:7

Cast your cares on the Lord and he will sustain you; he will never let the righteous fall.

Psalm 55:22

Record my lament; list my tears on your scroll — are they not in your record?

Then my enemies will turn back when I call for help. By this I will know that God is for me.

In God, whose word I praise, in the Lord, whose word I praise.

Psalm 56:8-10

My comfort in my suffering is this: Your promise preserves my life.

Psalm 119:50

I remember your ancient laws, O Lord, and I find comfort in them.

Psalm 119:52

Your decrees are the theme of my song wherever I lodge.

Psalm 119:54

Bible Promises for Encouragement

Have I not commanded you? Be strong and courageous. Do not be terrified; do not be discouraged, for the Lord your God will be with you wherever you go.

Joshua 1:9

But thanks be to God, who always leads us in triumphal procession in Christ and through us spreads everywhere the fragrance of the knowledge of him.

2 Corinthians 2:14

Being confident of this, that he who began a good work in you will carry it on to completion until the day of Christ Jesus.

Philippians 1:6

When I called, you answered me; you made me bold and stouthearted.

Psalm 138:3

Though I walk in the midst of trouble, you preserve my life; you stretch out your hand against the anger of my foes, with your right hand you save me.

The Lord will fulfill [his purpose] for me; your love, O Lord, endures forever — do not abandon the works of your hands.

Psalm 138:7,8

But you, O Lord, have mercy on me; raise me up, that I may repay them.

Psalm 41:10

When you pass through the waters, I will be with you; and when you pass through the rivers, they will not sweep over you. When you walk through the fire, you will not be burned; the flames will not set you ablaze.

Isaiah 43:2

The Lord will surely comfort Zion and will look with compassion on all her ruins; he will make her deserts like Eden, her wastelands like the garden of the Lord. Joy and gladness will be found in her, thanksgiving and the sound of singing.

Isaiah 51:3

I, even I, am he who comforts you. Who are you that you fear mortal men, the sons of men, who are but grass.

Isaiah 51:12

The Lord will fulfill [his purpose] for me; your love, O Lord, endures forever — do not abandon the works of your hands.

Psalm 138:8

"For I know the plans I have for you," declares the Lord, "plans to prosper you and not to harm you, plans to give you hope and a future."

Jeremiah 29:11

May our Lord Jesus Christ himself and God our Father, who loved us and by his grace gave us eternal encouragement and good hope,

Encourage your hearts and strengthen you in every good deed and word.

2 Thessalonians 2:16,17

God is not unjust; he will not forget your work and the love you have shown him as you have helped his people and continue to help them.

We want each of you to show this same diligence to the very end, in order to make your hope sure.

We do not want you to become lazy, but to imitate those who through faith and patience inherit what has been promised.

Hebrews 6:10-12

But from everlasting to everlasting the Lord's love is with those who fear him, and his righteousness with their children's children.

Psalm 103:17

Be strong and courageous. Do not be afraid or terrified because of them, for the Lord your God goes with you; he will never leave you nor forsake you.

Deuteronomy 31:6

Yet I am always with you; you hold me by my right hand.

Psalm 73:23

So he said to me, "This is the word of the Lord to Zerubbabel: "Not by might nor by power, but by my Spirit," says the Lord Almighty.

Zechariah 4:6

Trust in the Lord and do good; dwell in the land and enjoy safe pasture.

Delight yourself in the Lord and he will give you the desires of your heart.

Commit your way to the Lord; trust in him and he will do this.

Psalm 37:3-5

Praise our God, O peoples, let the sound of his praise be heard.

He has preserved our lives and kept our feet from slipping.

Psalm 66:8,9

I will praise God's name in song and glorify him with thanksgiving.

Psalm 69:30

The poor will see and be glad — you who seek God, may your hearts live!

Psalm 69:32

The path of the righteous is like the first gleam of dawn, shining ever brighter till the full light of day.

Proverbs 4:18

Bible Promises for Faith

Consequently, faith comes from hearing the message, and the message is heard through the word of Christ.

Romans 10:17

But what does it say? "The word is near you; it is in your mouth and in your heart," that is, the word of faith we are proclaiming.

Romans 10:8

The Lord is a refuge for the oppressed, a stronghold in times of trouble.

Those who know your name will trust in you, for you, Lord, have never forsaken those who seek you.

Psalm 9:9,10

It is better to take refuge in the Lord than to trust in man.

It is better to take refuge in the Lord than to trust in princes.

Psalm 118:8,9

As for God, his way is perfect; the word of the Lord is flawless. He is a shield for all who take refuge in him.

2 Samuel 22:31

Those who trust in the Lord are like Mount Zion, which cannot be shaken but endures forever.

Psalm 125:1

My help comes from the Lord, the Maker of heaven and earth.

He will not let your foot slip — he who watches over you will not slumber;

Indeed, he who watches over Israel will neither slumber nor sleep.

Psalm 121:2-4

But let all who take refuge in you be glad; let them ever sing for joy. Spread your protection over them, that those who love your name may rejoice in you.

Psalm 5:11

May the God of hope fill you with all joy and peace as you trust in him, so that you may overflow with hope by the power of the Holy Spirit.

Romans 15:13

And we also thank God continually because, when you received the word of God, which you heard from us, you accepted it not as the word of men, but as it actually is, the word of God, which is at work in you who believe.

1 Thessalonians 2:13

But my righteous one will live by faith. And if he shrinks back, I will not be pleased with him.

But we are not of those who shrink back and are destroyed, but of those who believe and are saved.

Hebrews 10:38,39

For everyone born of God overcomes the world. This is the victory that has overcome the world, even our faith.

1 John 5:4

The Lord himself goes before you and will be with you; he will never leave you nor forsake you. Do not be afraid; do not be discouraged.

Deuteronomy 31:8

Early in the morning they left for the Desert of Tekoa. As they set out, Jehoshaphat stood and said, "Listen to me, Judah and people of Jerusalem! Have faith in the Lord your God and you will be upheld; have faith in his prophets and you will be successful."

2 Chronicles 20:20

"Be strong and courageous. Do not be afraid or discouraged because of the king of Assyria and the vast army with him, for there is a greater power with us than with him.

With him is only the arm of flesh, but with us is the Lord our God to help us and to fight our battles." And the people gained confidence from what Hezekiah the king of Judah said.

2 Chronicles 32:7,8

Be not afraid, O land; be glad and rejoice. Surely the Lord has done great things.

Joel 2:21

See, he is puffed up; his desires are not upright — but the righteous will live by his faith.

Habakkuk 2:4

David also said to Solomon his son, "Be strong and courageous, and do the work. Do not be afraid or discouraged, for the Lord God, my God, is with you. He will not fail you or forsake you until all the work for the service of the temple of the Lord is finished.

1 Chronicles 28:20

The Lord is my shepherd, I shall not be in want.

Psalm 23:1

Bible Promises for Finances

And my God will meet all your needs according to his glorious riches in Christ Jesus.

Philippians 4:19

Remember this: Whoever sows sparingly will also reap sparingly, and whoever sows generously will also reap generously.

Each man should give what he has decided in his heart to give, not reluctantly or under compulsion, for God loves a cheerful giver.

And God is able to make all grace abound to you, so that in all things at all times, having all that you need, you will abound in every good work.

As it is written: "He has scattered abroad his gifts to the poor; his righteousness endures forever."

Now he who supplies seed to the sower and bread for food will also supply and increase your store of seed and will enlarge the harvest of your righteousness.

2 Corinthians 9:6-10

I answered them by saying, "The God of heaven will give us success. We his servants will start rebuilding, but as for you, you have no share in Jerusalem or any claim or historic right to it."

Nehemiah 2:20

Therefore I tell you, do not worry about your life, what you will eat or drink; or about your body, what you will wear. Is not life more important than food, and the body more important than clothes?

Look at the birds of the air; they do not sow or reap or store away in barns, and yet your heavenly Father feeds them. Are you not much more valuable than they?

Who of you by worrying can add a single hour to his life?

And why do you worry about clothes? See how the lilies of the field grow. They do not labor or spin.

Yet I tell you that not even Solomon in all his splendor was dressed like one of these.

If that is how God clothes the grass of the field, which is here today and tomorrow is thrown into the fire, will he not much more clothe you, O you of little faith?

So do not worry, saying, "What shall we eat?" or "What shall we drink?" or "What shall we wear?"

For the pagans run after all these things, and your heavenly Father knows that you need them.

But seek first his kingdom and his righteousness, and all these things will be given to you as well.

Therefore do not worry about tomorrow, for tomorrow will worry about itself. Each day has enough trouble of its own.

Matthew 6:25-34

For you know the grace of our Lord Jesus Christ, that though he was rich, yet for your sakes he became poor, so that you through his poverty might become rich.

2 Corinthians 8:9

As it is written: "He who gathered much did not have too much, and he who gathered little did not have too little."

2 Corinthians 8:15

He who has been stealing must steal no longer, but must work, doing something useful with his own hands, that he may have something to share with those in need.

Ephesians 4:28

Give, and it will be given to you. A good measure, pressed down, shaken together and running over, will be poured into your lap. For with the measure you use, it will be measured to you.

Luke 6:38

Do not be deceived: God cannot be mocked. A man reaps what he sows.

Galatians 6:7

I was young and now I am old, yet I have never seen the righteous forsaken or their children begging bread.

They are always generous and lend freely; their children will be blessed.

Psalm 37:25,26

"Bring the whole tithe into the storehouse, that there may be food in my house. Test me in this," says the Lord Almighty, "and see if I will not throw open the floodgates of heaven and pour out so much blessing that you will not have room enough for it.

"I will prevent pests from devouring your crops, and the vines in your fields will not cast their fruit," says the Lord Almighty.

"Then all the nations will call you blessed, for yours will be a delightful land," says the Lord Almighty.

Malachi 3:10-12

Honor the Lord with your wealth, with the firstfruits of all your crops;

Then your barns will be filled to overflowing, and your vats will brim over with new wine.

Proverbs 3:9,10

"'If you can'?" said Jesus. "Everything is possible for him who believes."

Mark 9:23

Cast your bread upon the waters, for after many days you will find it again.

Ecclesiastes 11:1

The Lord does not let the righteous go hungry but he thwarts the craving of the wicked.

Proverbs 10:3

This is what the Lord says — your Redeemer, the Holy One of Israel: "I am the Lord your God, who teaches you what is best for you, who directs you in the way you should go."

Isaiah 48:17

Bible Promises for Forgiving Others

Be imitators of God, therefore, as dearly loved children

And live a life of love, just as Christ loved us and gave himself up for us as a fragrant offering and sacrifice to God.

Ephesians 5:1,2

"In your anger do not sin": Do not let the sun go down while you are still angry,

And do not give the devil a foothold.

Ephesians 4:26,27

Forgive us our debts, as we also have forgiven our debtors.

Matthew 6:12

For if you forgive men when they sin against you, your heavenly Father will also forgive you.

But if you do not forgive men their sins, your Father will not forgive your sins.

Matthew 6:14,15

Giving thanks to the Father, who has qualified you to share in the inheritance of the saints in the kingdom of light.

For he has rescued us from the dominion of darkness and brought us into the kingdom of the Son he loves,

In whom we have redemption, the forgiveness of sins.

He is the image of the invisible God, the firstborn over all creation.

For by him all things were created: things in heaven and on earth, visible and invisible, whether thrones or powers or rulers or authorities; all things were created by him and for him.

He is before all things, and in him all things hold together.

Colossians 1:12-17

Make every effort to live in peace with all men and to be holy; without holiness no one will see the Lord.

See to it that no one misses the grace of God and that no bitter root grows up to cause trouble and defile many.

Hebrews 12:14,15

Love is patient, love is kind. It does not envy, it does not boast, it is not proud.

It is not rude, it is not self-seeking, it is not easily angered, it keeps no record of wrongs.

Love does not delight in evil but rejoices with the truth.

It always protects, always trusts, always hopes, always perseveres.

Love never fails.

1 Corinthians 13:4-8a

A man's wisdom gives him patience; it is to his glory to overlook an offense.

Proverbs 19:11

If you come across your enemy's ox or donkey wandering off, be sure to take it back to him.

If you see the donkey of someone who hates you fallen down under its load, do not leave it there; be sure you help him with it.

Exodus 23:4,5

Blessed are the merciful, for they will be shown mercy.

Matthew 5:7

But I tell you, Do not resist an evil person. If someone strikes you on the right cheek, turn to him the other also.

And if someone wants to sue you and take your tunic, let him have your cloak as well.

If someone forces you to go one mile, go with him two miles.

Give to the one who asks you, and do not turn away from the one who wants to borrow from you.

You have heard that it was said, "Love your neighbor and hate your enemy."

But I tell you: Love your enemies and pray for those who persecute you,

That you may be sons of your Father in heaven. He causes his sun to rise on the evil and the good, and sends rain on the righteous and the unrighteous.

If you love those who love you, what reward will you get? Are not even the tax collectors doing that?

Matthew 5:39-46

And when you stand praying, if you hold anything against anyone, forgive him, so that your Father in heaven may forgive you your sins.

Mark 11:25

But love your enemies, do good to them, and lend to them without expecting to get anything back. Then your reward will be great, and you will be sons of the Most High, because he is kind to the ungrateful and wicked.

Be merciful, just as your Father is merciful.

Do not judge, and you will not be judged. Do not condemn, and you will not be condemned. Forgive, and you will be forgiven.

Luke 6:35-37

So watch yourselves. "If your brother sins, rebuke him, and if he repents, forgive him.

"If he sins against you seven times in a day, and seven times comes back to you and says, 'I repent,' forgive him."

Luke 17:3,4

Bless those who persecute you; bless and do not curse.

Romans 12:14

Do not repay anyone evil for evil. Be careful to do what is right in the eyes of everybody.

Romans 12:17

Do not take revenge, my friends, but leave room for God's wrath, for it is written: "It is mine to avenge; I will repay," says the Lord.

Romans 12:19

Do not be overcome by evil, but overcome evil with good.

Romans 12:21

To be made new in the attitude of your minds.

Ephesians 4:23

Do not repay evil with evil or insult with insult, but with blessing, because to this you were called so that you may inherit a blessing.

1 Peter 3:9

Bible Promises for Good Health

Surely he took up our infirmities and carried our sorrows, yet we considered him stricken by God, smitten by him, and afflicted.

But he was pierced for our transgressions, he was crushed for our iniquities; the punishment that brought us peace was upon him, and by his wounds we are healed.

Isaiah 53:4,5

Christ redeemed us from the curse of the law by becoming a curse for us, for it is written: "Cursed is everyone who is hung on a tree."

Galatians 3:13

Worship the Lord your God, and his blessing will be on your food and water. I will take away sickness from among you,

And none will miscarry or be barren in your land. I will give you a full life span.

Exodus 23:25,26

When evening came, many who were demon-possessed were brought to him, and he drove out the spirits with a word and healed all the sick.

This was to fulfill what was spoken through the prophet Isaiah: "He took up our infirmities and carried our diseases."

Matthew 8:16,17

He himself bore our sins in his body on the tree, so that we might die to sins and live for righteousness; by his wounds you have been healed.

1 Peter 2:24

He said, "If you listen carefully to the voice of the Lord your God and do what is right in his eyes, if you pay attention to his commands and keep all his decrees, I will not bring on you any of the diseases I brought on the Egyptians, for I am the Lord, who heals you."

Exodus 15:26

Then no harm will befall you, no disaster will come near your tent.

Psalm 91:10

With long life will I satisfy him and show him my salvation.

Psalm 91:16

Praise the Lord, O my soul, and 'orget not all his benefits —

Who forgives all your sins and heals all your diseases.

Psalm 103:2,3

He sent forth his word and healed them; he rescued them from the grave.

Psalm 107:20

So is my word that goes out from my mouth: It will not return to me empty, but will accomplish what I desire and achieve the purpose for which I sent it.

Isaiah 55:11

Every good and perfect gift is from above, coming down from the Father of the heavenly lights, who does not change like shifting shadows.

James 1:17

A man with leprosy came and knelt before him and said, "Lord, if you are willing, you can make me clean."

Jesus reached out his hand and touched the man. "I am willing," he said. "Be clean!" Immediately he was cured of his leprosy.

Matthew 8:2,3

How God anointed Jesus of Nazareth with the Holy Spirit and power, and how he went around doing good and healing all who were under the power of the devil, because God was with him.

Acts 10:38

The thief comes only to steal and kill and destroy; I have come that they may have life, and have it to the full.

John 10:10

Jesus Christ is the same yesterday and today and forever.

Hebrews 13:8

I tell you the truth, anyone who has faith in me will do what I have been doing. He will do even greater things than these, because I am going to the Father.

John 14:12

Is any one of you sick? He should call the elders of the church to pray over him and anoint him with oil in the name of the Lord.

And the prayer offered in faith will make the sick person well; the Lord will raise him up. If he has sinned, he will be forgiven.

James 5:14,15

Dear friend, I pray that you may enjoy good health and that all may go well with you, even as your soul is getting along well.

3 John 2

You, dear children, are from God and have overcome them, because the one who is in you is greater than the one who is in the world.

1 John 4:4

I tell you the truth, if anyone says to this mountain, "Go, throw yourself into the sea," and does not doubt in his heart but believes that what he says will happen, it will be done for him.

Therefore I tell you, whatever you ask for in prayer, believe that you have received it, and it will be yours.

Mark 11:23,24

Bible Promises for Joy

I have told you this so that my joy may be in you and that your joy may be complete.

John 15:11

I will be glad and rejoice in you; I will sing praise to your name, O Most High.

Psalm 9:2

Then my soul will rejoice in the Lord and delight in his salvation.

Psalm 35:9

The Lord is my strength and my shield; my heart trusts in him, and I am helped. My heart leaps for joy and I will give thanks to him in song.

Psalm 28:7

You have made known to me the path of life; you will fill me with joy in your presence, with eternal pleasures at your right hand.

Psalm 16:11

Splendor and majesty are before him; strength and joy in his dwelling place.

1 Chronicles 16:27

And on that day they offered great sacrifices, rejoicing because God had given them great joy. The women and children also rejoiced. The sound of rejoicing in Jerusalem could be heard far away.

Nehemiah 12:43

You have filled my heart with greater joy than when their grain and new wine abound.

Psalm 4:7

The precepts of the Lord are right, giving joy to the heart. The commands of the Lord are radiant, giving light to the eyes.

Psalm 19:8

Will you not revive us again, that your people may rejoice in you?

Psalm 85:6

Blessed are those who have learned to acclaim you, who walk in the light of your presence, O Lord.

They rejoice in your name all day long; they exult in your righteousness.

Psalm 89:15,16

Shout for joy to the Lord, all the earth.

Worship the Lord with gladness; come before him with joyful songs.

Psalm 100:1,2

When the Lord brought back the captives to Zion, we were like men who dreamed.

Our mouths were filled with laughter, our tongues with songs of joy. Then it was said among the nations, "The Lord has done great things for them."

Psalm 126:1,2

When your words came, I ate them; they were my joy and my heart's delight, for I bear your name, O Lord God Almighty.

Jeremiah 15:16

However, do not rejoice that the spirits submit to you, but rejoice that your names are written in heaven.

Luke 10:20

You have made known to me the paths of life; you will fill me with joy in your presence.

Acts 2:28

And the disciples were filled with joy and with the Holy Spirit.

Acts 13:52

For the kingdom of God is not a matter of eating and drinking, but of righteousness, peace and joy in the Holy Spirit.

Romans 14:17

For you were once darkness, but now you are light in the Lord. Live as children of light.

Ephesians 5:8

Whatever you have learned or received or heard from me, or seen in me — put it into practice. And the God of peace will be with you.

Philippians 4:9

Though you have not seen him, you love him; and even though you do not see him now, you believe in him and are filled with an inexpressible and glorious joy.

1 Peter 1:8

Bible Promises for Love

This is love: not that we loved God, but that he loved us and sent his Son as an atoning sacrifice for our sins.

Dear friends, since God so loved us, we also ought to love one another.

No one has ever seen God; but if we love one another, God lives in us and his love is made complete in us.

1 John 4:10-12

And so we know and rely on the love God has for us. God is love. Whoever lives in love lives in God, and God in him.

In this way, love is made complete among us so that we will have confidence on the day of judgment, because in this world we are like him.

There is no fear in love. But perfect love drives out fear, because fear has to do with punishment. The one who fears is not made perfect in love.

1 John 4:16-18

And this is my prayer: that your love may abound more and more in knowledge and depth of insight,

So that you may be able to discern what is best and may be pure and blameless until the day of Christ,

Filled with the fruit of righteousness that comes through Jesus Christ — to the glory and praise of God.

Philippians 1:9-11

And hope does not disappoint us, because God has poured out his love into our hearts by the Holy Spirit, whom he has given us.

Romans 5:5

May the Lord make your love increase and overflow for each other and for everyone else, just as ours does for you.

May he strengthen your hearts so that you will be blameless and holy in the presence of our God and Father when our Lord Jesus comes with all his holy ones.

1 Thessalonians 3:12,13

Now about brotherly love we do not need to write to you, for you yourselves have been taught by God to love each other.

And in fact, you do love all the brothers throughout Macedonia. Yet we urge you, brothers, to do so more and more.

1 Thessalonians 4:9,10

May the Lord direct your hearts into God's love and Christ's perseverance.

2 Thessalonians 3:5

Hatred stirs up dissension, but love covers over all wrongs.

Proverbs 10:12

Place me like a seal over your heart, like a seal on your arm; for love is as strong as death, its jealousy unyielding as the grave. It burns like blazing fire, like a mighty flame.

Many waters cannot quench love; rivers cannot wash it away. If one were to give all the wealth of his house for love, it would be utterly scorned.

Song of Songs 8:6,7

A friend loves at all times, and a brother is born for adversity.

Proverbs 17:17

"Honor your father and mother," and "love your neighbor as yourself."

Matthew 19:19

Love the Lord your God with all your heart and with all your soul and with all your strength.

Deuteronomy 6:5

And now, O Israel, what does the Lord your God ask of you but to fear the Lord your God, to walk in all his ways, to love him, to serve the Lord your God with all your heart and with all your soul.

Deuteronomy 10:12

But be very careful to keep the commandment and the law that Moses the servant of the Lord gave you: to love the Lord your God, to walk in all his ways, to obey his commands, to hold fast to him and to serve him with all your heart and all your soul.

Joshua 22:5

I love the Lord, for he heard my voice; he heard my cry for mercy.

Psalm 116:1

A new command I give you: Love one another. As I have loved you, so you must love one another.

By this all men will know that you are my disciples, if you love one another.

John 13:34,35

Now about food sacrificed to idols: We know that we all possess knowledge. Knowledge puffs up, but love builds up.

1 Corinthians 8:1

The goal of this command is love, which comes from a pure heart and a good conscience and a sincere faith.

1 Timothy 1:5

Above all, love each other deeply, because love covers over a multitude of sins.

1 Peter 4:8

Whoever loves his brother lives in the light, and there is nothing in him to make him stumble.

1 John 2:10

Bible Promises for Motivation

Do you see a man skilled in his work? He will serve before kings; he will not serve before obscure men.

Proverbs 22:29

Make it your ambition to lead a quiet life, to mind your own business and to work with your hands, just as we told you,

So that your daily life may win the respect of outsiders and so that you will not be dependent on anybody.

1 Thessalonians 4:11,12

Lazy hands make a man poor, but diligent hands bring wealth.

Proverbs 10:4

Never be lacking in zeal, but keep your spiritual fervor, serving the Lord.

Romans 12:11

Slaves, obey your earthly masters in everything; and do it, not only when their eye is on you and to win their favor, but with sincerity of heart and reverence for the Lord.

Whatever you do, work at it with all your heart, as working for the Lord, not for men.

Colossians 3:22,23

Stay in that house, eating and drinking whatever they give you, for the worker deserves his wages. Do not move around from house to house.

Luke 10:7

For this reason I remind you to fan into flame the gift of God, which is in you through the laying on of my hands.

For God did not give us a spirit of timidity, but a spirit of power, of love and of self-discipline.

2 Timothy 1:6,7

But the men of Israel encouraged one another and again took up their positions where they had stationed themselves the first day.

Judges 20:22

Diligent hands will rule, but laziness ends in slave labor.

Proverbs 12:24

I walk in the way of righteousness, along the paths of justice,

Bestowing wealth on those who love me and making their treasuries full.

Proverbs 8:20,21

Laziness brings on deep sleep, and the shiftless man goes hungry.

Proverbs 19:15

He who gathers crops in summer is a wise son, but he who sleeps during harvest is a disgraceful son.

Proverbs 10:5

He who works his land will have abundant food, but he who chases fantasies lacks judgment.

Proverbs 12:11

Dishonest money dwindles away, but he who gathers money little by little makes it grow.

Proverbs 13:11

Do not love sleep or you will grow poor; stay awake and you will have food to spare.

Proverbs 20:13

For even when we were with you, we gave you this rule: If a man will not work, he shall not eat.

2 Thessalonians 3:10

We do not want you to become lazy, but to imitate those who through faith and patience inherit what has been promised.

Hebrews 6:12

If a man is lazy, the rafters sag; if his hands are idle, the house leaks.

Ecclesiastes 10:18

No, in all these things we are more than conquerors through him who loved us.

Romans 8:37

Bible Promises for Patience

You need to persevere so that when you have done the will of God, you will receive what he has promised.

Hebrews 10:36

Be still before the Lord and wait patiently for him; do not fret when men succeed in their ways, when they carry out their wicked schemes.

Refrain from anger and turn from wrath; do not fret — it leads only to evil.

For evil men will be cut off, but those who hope in the Lord will inherit the land.

Psalm 37:7-9

But you, man of God, flee from all this, and pursue righteousness, godliness, faith, love, endurance and gentleness.

1 Timothy 6:11

We do not want you to become lazy, but to imitate those who through faith and patience inherit what has been promised.

Hebrews 6:12

The end of a matter is better than its beginning, and patience is better than pride.

Do not be quickly provoked in your spirit, for anger resides in the lap of fools.

Ecclesiastes 7:8,9

By standing firm you will gain life.

Luke 21:19

Not only so, but we also rejoice in our sufferings, because we know that suffering produces perseverance.

Romans 5:3

Let us not become weary in doing good, for at the proper time we will reap a harvest if we do not give up.

Galatians 6:9

As a prisoner for the Lord, then, I urge you to live a life worthy of the calling you have received.

Ephesians 4:1

Be completely humble and gentle; be patient, bearing with one another in love.

Ephesians 4:2

And we pray this in order that you may live a life worthy of the Lord and may please him in every way: bearing fruit in every good work, growing in the knowledge of God,

Being strengthened with all power according to his glorious might so that you may have great endurance and patience, and joyfully.

Colossians 1:10,11

And we urge you, brothers, warn those who are idle, encourage the timid, help the weak, be patient with everyone.

1 Thessalonians 5:14

May the Lord direct your hearts into God's love and Christ's perseverance.

2 Thessalonians 3:5

And so after waiting patiently, Abraham received what was promised.

Hebrews 6:15

Therefore, since we are surrounded by such a great cloud of witnesses, let us throw off everything that hinders and the sin that so easily entangles, and let us run with perseverance the race marked out for us.

Hebrews 12:1

Because you know that the testing of your faith develops perseverance.

Perseverance must finish its work so that you may be mature and complete, not lacking anything.

James 1:3,4

My dear brothers, take note of this: Everyone should be quick to listen, slow to speak and slow to become angry.

James 1:19

Be patient, then, brothers, until the Lord's coming. See how the farmer waits for the land to yield its valuable crop and how patient he is for the autumn and spring rains.

You too, be patient and stand firm, because the Lord's coming is near.

James 5:7,8

For this very reason, make every effort to add to your faith goodness; and to goodness, knowledge;

And to knowledge, self-control; and to self-control, perseverance; and to perseverance, godliness.

2 Peter 1:5,6

This calls for patient endurance on the part of the saints who obey God's commandments and remain faithful to Jesus.

Revelation 14:12

The Lord is not slow in keeping his promise, as some understand slowness. He is patient with you, not wanting anyone to perish, but everyone to come to repentance.

2 Peter 3:9

Bible Promises for Peace

Blessed are the peacemakers, for they will be called sons of God.

Matthew 5:9

You will keep in perfect peace him whose mind is steadfast, because he trusts in you.

Trust in the Lord forever, for the Lord, the Lord, is the Rock eternal.

Isaiah 26:3,4

I will listen to what God the Lord will say; he promises peace to his people, his saints — but let them not return to folly.

Psalm 85:8

Now may the Lord of peace himself give you peace at all times and in every way. The Lord be with all of you.

2 Thessalonians 3:16

When a man's ways are pleasing to the Lord, he makes even his enemies live at peace with him.

Proverbs 16:7

It is to a man's honor to avoid strife, but every fool is quick to quarrel.

Proverbs 20:3

Also, seek the peace and prosperity of the city to which I have carried you into exile. Pray to the Lord for it, because if it prospers, you too will prosper.

Jeremiah 29:7

Submit to God and be at peace with him; in this way prosperity will come to you.

Job 22:21

Lord, you establish peace for us; all that we have accomplished you have done for us.

Isaiah 26:12

Who, then, is the man that fears the Lord? He will instruct him in the way chosen for him.

He will spend his days in prosperity, and his descendants will inherit the land.

Psalm 25:12,13

Consider the blameless, observe the upright; there is a future for the man of peace.

Psalm 37:37

Great peace have they who love your law, and nothing can make them stumble.

Psalm 119:165

Those who trust in the Lord are like Mount Zion, which cannot be shaken but endures forever.

Psalm 125:1

To whom he said, "This is the resting place, let the weary rest"; and, "This is the place of repose" — but they would not listen.

Isaiah 28:12

"The glory of this present house will be greater than the glory of the former house," says the Lord Almighty. "And in this place I will grant peace," declares the Lord Almighty.

Haggai 2:9

My covenant was with him, a covenant of life and peace, and I gave them to him; this called for reverence and he revered me and stood in awe of my name.

Malachi 2:5

To shine on those living in darkness and in the shadow of death, to guide our feet into the path of peace.

Luke 1:79

Peace I leave with you; my peace I give you. I do not give to you as the world gives. Do not let your hearts be troubled and do not be afraid.

John 14:27

Therefore, since we have been justified through faith, we have peace with God through our Lord Jesus Christ.

Romans 5:1

For the kingdom of God is not a matter of eating and drinking, but of righteousness, peace and joy in the Holy Spirit.

Romans 14:17

Do not be anxious about anything, but in everything, by prayer and petition, with thanksgiving, present your requests to God.

And the peace of God, which transcends all understanding, will guard your hearts and your minds in Christ Jesus.

Philippians 4:6,7

Let the peace of Christ rule in your hearts, since as members of one body you were called to peace. And be thankful.

Colossians 3:15

He ransoms me unharmed from the battle waged against me, even though many oppose me.

Psalm 55:18

Bible Promises for Protection

Therefore let everyone who is godly pray to you while you may be found; surely when the mighty waters rise, they will not reach him.

You are my hiding place; you will protect me from trouble and surround me with songs of deliverance. *Selah*

Psalm 32:6,7

He who dwells in the shelter of the Most High will rest in the shadow of the Almighty.

I will say of the Lord, "He is my refuge and my fortress, my God, in whom I trust."

Surely he will save you from the fowler's snare and from the deadly pestilence.

He will cover you with his feathers, and under his wings you will find refuge; his faithfulness will be your shield and rampart.

You will not fear the terror of night, nor the arrow that flies by day,

Nor the pestilence that stalks in the darkness, nor the plague that destroys at midday.

A thousand may fall at your side, ten thousand at your right hand, but it will not come near you.

You will only observe with your eyes and see the punishment of the wicked.

If you make the Most High your dwelling — even the Lord, who is my refuge —

Then no harm will befall you, no disaster will come near your tent.

For he will command his angels concerning you to guard you in all your ways;

They will lift you up in their hands, so that you will not strike your foot against a stone.

You will tread upon the lion and the cobra; you will trample the great lion and the serpent.

"Because he loves me," says the Lord, "I will rescue him; I will protect him, for he acknowledges my name.

He will call upon me, and I will answer him; I will be with him in trouble, I will deliver him and honor him.

With long life will I satisfy him and show him my salvation."

Psalm 91:1-16

"And I myself will be a wall of fire around it," declares the Lord, "and I will be its glory within."

Zechariah 2:5

That is why I am suffering as I am. Yet I am not ashamed, because I know whom I have believed, and am convinced that he is able to guard what I have entrusted to him for that day.

2 Timothy 1:12

God is our refuge and strength, an ever-present help in trouble.

Therefore we will not fear, though the earth give way and the mountains fall into the heart of the sea.

Psalm 46:1,2

God is within her, she will not fall; God will help her at break of day.

Psalm 46:5

When I am afraid, I will trust in you.

In God, whose word I praise, in God I trust; I will not be afraid. What can mortal man do to me?

Psalm 56:3,4

Give us aid against the enemy, for the help of man is worthless.

With God we will gain the victory, and he will trample down our enemies.

Psalm 60:11,12

Hear my cry, O God; listen to my prayer.

From the ends of the earth I call to you, I call as my heart grows faint; lead me to the rock that is higher than I.

For you have been my refuge, a strong tower against the foe.

I long to dwell in your tent forever and take refuge in the shelter of your wings. *Selah*

Psalm 61:1-4

He who fears the Lord has a secure fortress, and for his children it will be a refuge.

The fear of the Lord is a fountain of life, turning a man from the snares of death.

Proverbs 14:26,27

As for God, his way is perfect; the word of the Lord is flawless. He is a shield for all who take refuge in him.

2 Samuel 22:31

To him who is able to keep you from falling and to present you before his glorious presence without fault and with great joy.

Jude 24

Bible Promises for Self-Control

So I say, live by the Spirit, and you will not gratify the desires of the sinful nature.

Galatians 5:16

Therefore, since Christ suffered in his body, arm yourselves also with the same attitude, because he who has suffered in his body is done with sin.

As a result, he does not live the rest of his earthly life for evil human desires, but rather for the will of God.

1 Peter 4:1,2

Let your gentleness be evident to all. The Lord is near.

Philippians 4:5

For we know that our old self was crucified with him so that the body of sin might be done away with, that we should no longer be slaves to sin.

Romans 6:6

Rather, clothe yourselves with the Lord Jesus Christ, and do not think about how to gratify the desires of the sinful nature.

Romans 13:14

And put a knife to your throat if you are given to gluttony.

Proverbs 23:2

Better a patient man than a warrior, a man who controls his temper than one who takes a city.

Proverbs 16:32

"Everything is permissible for me" — but not everything is beneficial. "Everything is permissible for me" — but I will not be mastered by anything.

1 Corinthians 6:12

I have been crucified with Christ and I no longer live, but Christ lives in me. The life I live in the body, I live by faith in the Son of God, who loved me and gave himself for me.

Galatians 2:20

Those who belong to Christ Jesus have crucified the sinful nature with its passions and desires.

Galatians 5:24

No one serving as a soldier gets involved in civilian affairs — he wants to please his commanding officer.

2 Timothy 2:4

Dear friends, I urge you, as aliens and strangers in the world, to abstain from sinful desires, which war against your soul.

1 Peter 2:11

If you find honey, eat just enough — too much of it, and you will vomit.

Proverbs 25:16

Everyone who competes in the games goes into strict training. They do it to get a crown that will not last; but we do it to get a crown that will last forever.

Therefore I do not run like a man running aimlessly; I do not fight like a man beating the air.

No, I beat my body and make it my slave so that after I have preached to others, I myself will not be disqualified for the prize.

1 Corinthians 9:25-27

Bible Promises for Strength

The Lord is my strength and my song; he has become my salvation. He is my God, and I will praise him, my father's God, and I will exalt him.

Exodus 15:2

He gives strength to the weary and increases the power of the weak.

Isaiah 40:29

Summon your power, O God; show us your strength, O God, as you have done before.

Psalm 68:28

Finally, be strong in the Lord and in his mighty power.

Ephesians 6:10

All his laws are before me; I have not turned away from his decrees.

2 Samuel 22:23

The Lord is my strength and my song; he has become my salvation.

Psalm 118:14

Surely God is my salvation; I will trust and not be afraid. The Lord, the Lord, is my strength and my song; he has become my salvation.

Isaiah 12:2

You armed me with strength for battle; you made my adversaries bow at my feet.

2 Samuel 22:40

It is God who arms me with strength and makes my way perfect.

Psalm 18:32

You armed me with strength for battle; you made my adversaries bow at my feet.

Psalm 18:39

May the words of my mouth and the meditation of my heart be pleasing in your sight, O Lord, my Rock and my Redeemer.

Psalm 19:14

The Lord gives strength to his people; the Lord blesses his people with peace.

Psalm 29:11

Sing for joy to God our strength; shout aloud to the God of Jacob!

Psalm 81:1

My flesh and my heart may fail, but God is the strength of my heart and my portion forever.

Psalm 73:26

A wise man has great power, and a man of knowledge increases strength.

Proverbs 24:5

Trust in the Lord forever, for the Lord, the Lord, is the Rock eternal.

Isaiah 26:4

But he said to me, "My grace is sufficient for you, for my power is made perfect in weakness." Therefore I will boast all the more gladly about my weaknesses, so that Christ's power may rest on me.

2 Corinthians 12:9

Bible Promises for Wisdom

If any of you lacks wisdom, he should ask God, who gives generously to all without finding fault, and it will be given to him.

But when he asks, he must believe and not doubt, because he who doubts is like a wave of the sea, blown and tossed by the wind.

That man should not think he will receive anything from the Lord;

He is a double-minded man, unstable in all he does.

James 1:5-8

For this reason, since the day we heard about you, we have not stopped praying for you and asking God to fill you with the knowledge of his will through all spiritual wisdom and understanding.

Colossians 1:9

The unfolding of your words gives light; it gives understanding to the simple.

Psalm 119:130

Such "wisdom" does not come down from heaven but is earthly, unspiritual, of the devil.

For where you have envy and selfish ambition, there you find disorder and every evil practice.

But the wisdom that comes from heaven is first of all pure; then peace-loving, considerate, submissive, full of mercy and good fruit, impartial and sincere.

Peacemakers who sow in peace raise a harvest of righteousness.

James 3:15-18

I keep asking that the God of our Lord Jesus Christ, the glorious Father, may give you the Spirit of wisdom and revelation, so that you may know him better.

I pray also that the eyes of your heart may be enlightened in order that you may know the hope to which he has called you, the riches of his glorious inheritance in the saints,

And his incomparably great power for us who believe. That power is like the working of his mighty strength.

Ephesians 1:17-19

Call to me and I will answer you and tell you great and unsearchable things you do not know.

Jeremiah 33:3

But you have an anointing from the Holy One, and all of you know the truth.

1 John 2:20

As for you, the anointing you received from him remains in you, and you do not need anyone to teach you. But as his anointing teaches you about all things and as that anointing is real, not counterfeit — just as it has taught you, remain in him.

1 John 2:27

Whether you turn to the right or to the left, your ears will hear a voice behind you, saying, "This is the way; walk in it."

Isaiah 30:21

Do not bring hastily to court, for what will you do in the end if your neighbor puts you to shame?

If you argue your case with a neighbor, do not betray another man's confidence.

Proverbs 25:8,9

I will instruct you and teach you in the way you should go; I will counsel you and watch over you.

Psalm 32:8

For with you is the fountain of life; in your light we see light.

Psalm 36:9

If you had responded to my rebuke, I would have poured out my heart to you and made my thoughts known to you.

Proverbs 1:23

For the Lord gives wisdom, and from his mouth come knowledge and understanding.

He holds victory in store for the upright, he is a shield to those whose walk is blameless.

Proverbs 2:6,7

Send forth your light and your truth, let them guide me; let them bring me to your holy mountain, to the place where you dwell.

Psalm 43:3

Reflect on what I am saying, for the Lord will give you insight into all this.

2 Timothy 2:7

Bible Promises for Deliverance

I sought the Lord, and he answered me; he delivered me from all my fears.

Psalm 34:4

A righteous man may have many troubles, but the Lord delivers him from them all.

Psalm 34:19

One thing God has spoken, two things have I heard: that you, O God, are strong,

And that you, O Lord, are loving. Surely you will reward each person according to what he has done.

Psalm 62:11,12

If this is so, then the Lord knows how to rescue godly men from trials and to hold the unrighteous for the day of judgment, while continuing their punishment.

2 Peter 2:9

My soul finds rest in God alone; my salvation comes from him.

He alone is my rock and my salvation; he is my fortress, I will never be shaken.

Psalm 62:1,2

Find rest, O my soul, in God alone; my hope comes from him.

He alone is my rock and my salvation; he is my fortress, I will not be shaken.

My salvation and my honor depend on God; he is my mighty rock, my refuge.

Trust in him at all times, O people; pour out your hearts to him, for God is our refuge. *Selah*
Psalm 62:5-8

He reached down from on high and took hold of me; he drew me out of deep waters.

He rescued me from my powerful enemy, from my foes, who were too strong for me.

They confronted me in the day of my disaster, but the Lord was my support.

He brought me out into a spacious place; he rescued me because he delighted in me.
Psalm 18:16-19

In the shelter of your presence you hide them from the intrigues of men; in your dwelling you keep them safe from accusing tongues.

Psalm 31:20

To the Jews who had believed him, Jesus said, "If you hold to my teaching, you are really my disciples.

"Then you will know the truth, and the truth will set you free."

John 8:31,32

When Jesus had called the Twelve together, he gave them power and authority to drive out all demons and to cure diseases.

Luke 9:1

He called his twelve disciples to him and gave them authority to drive out evil spirits and to heal every disease and sickness.

Matthew 10:1

I have given you authority to trample on snakes and scorpions and to overcome all the power of the enemy; nothing will harm you.

Luke 10:19

When evening came, many who were demon-possessed were brought to him, and he drove out the spirits with a word and healed all the sick.

This was to fulfill what was spoken through the prophet Isaiah: "He took up our infirmities and carried our diseases."

Matthew 8:16,17

The Lord will rescue me from every evil attack and will bring me safely to his heavenly kingdom. To him be glory for ever and ever. Amen.

2 Timothy 4:18

Bible Promises for Guidance

Lead me, O Lord, in your righteousness because of my enemies — make straight your way before me.

Psalm 5:8

I will instruct you and teach you in the way you should go; I will counsel you and watch over you.

Psalm 32:8

You are my lamp, O Lord; the Lord turns my darkness into light.

2 Samuel 22:29

You guide me with your counsel, and afterward you will take me into glory.

Psalm 73:24

Because those who are led by the Spirit of God are sons of God.

Romans 8:14

The lamp of the Lord searches the spirit of a man; it searches out his inmost being.

Proverbs 20:27

The watchman opens the gate for him, and the sheep listen to his voice. He calls his own sheep by name and leads them out.

When he has brought out all his own, he goes on ahead of them, and his sheep follow him because they know his voice.

But they will never follow a stranger; in fact, they will run away from him because they do not recognize a stranger's voice.

John 10:3-5

In your unfailing love you will lead the people you have redeemed. In your strength you will guide them to your holy dwelling.

Exodus 15:13

In a desert land he found him, in a barren and howling waste. He shielded him and cared for him; he guarded him as the apple of his eye.

Deuteronomy 32:10

Because of your great compassion you did not abandon them in the desert. By day the pillar of cloud did not cease to guide them on their path, nor the pillar of fire by night to shine on the way they were to take.

You gave your good Spirit to instruct them. You did not withhold your manna from their mouths, and you gave them water for their thirst.

Nehemiah 9:19,20

He makes me lie down in green pastures, he leads me beside quiet waters,

He restores my soul. He guides me in paths of righteousness for his name's sake.

Psalm 23:2,3

Guide me in your truth and teach me, for you are God my Savior, and my hope is in you all day long.

Psalm 25:5

He guides the humble in what is right and teaches them his way.

Psalm 25:9

Teach me your way, O Lord; lead me in a straight path because of my oppressors.

Psalm 27:11

Since you are my rock and my fortress, for the sake of your name lead and guide me.

Psalm 31:3

For this God is our God for ever and ever; he will be our guide even to the end.

Psalm 48:14

From the ends of the earth I call to you, I call as my heart grows faint; lead me to the rock that is higher than I.

Psalm 61:2

If I rise on the wings of the dawn, if I settle on the far side of the sea,

Even there your hand will guide me, your right hand will hold me fast.

Psalm 139:9,10

See if there is any offensive way in me, and lead me in the way everlasting.

Psalm 139:24

I will lead the blind by ways they have not known, along unfamiliar paths I will guide them; I will turn the darkness into light before them and make the rough places smooth. These are the things I will do; I will not forsake them.

Isaiah 42:16

This is what the Lord says — your Redeemer, the Holy One of Israel: "I am the Lord your God, who teaches you what is best for you, who directs you in the way you should go."

Isaiah 48:17

The Lord will guide you always; he will satisfy your needs in a sun-scorched land and will strengthen your frame. You will be like a well-watered garden, like a spring whose waters never fail.

Isaiah 58:11

To shine on those living in darkness and in the shadow of death, to guide our feet into the path of peace.

Luke 1:79

But when he, the Spirit of truth, comes, he will guide you into all truth. He will not speak on his own; he will speak only what he hears, and he will tell you what is yet to come.

John 16:13

Because you know that the testing of your faith develops perseverance.

James 1:3

Call to me and I will answer you and tell you great and unsearchable things you do not know.

Jeremiah 33:3

7

GOD'S PURPOSE FOR YOUR LIFE

Witnessing and Enlarging
the Kingdom of God

He said to them, "Go into all the world and preach the good news to all creation."

Mark 16:15

I am not ashamed of the gospel, because it is the power of God for the salvation of everyone who believes: first for the Jew, then for the Gentile.

For in the gospel a righteousness from God is revealed, a righteousness that is by faith from first to last, just as it is written: "The righteous will live by faith."

Romans 1:16,17

We are therefore Christ's ambassadors, as though God were making his appeal through us. We implore you on Christ's behalf: Be reconciled to God.

2 Corinthians 5:20

And this gospel of the kingdom will be preached in the whole world as a testimony to all nations, and then the end will come.

Matthew 24:14

You are the light of the world. A city on a hill cannot be hidden.

Neither do people light a lamp and put it under a bowl. Instead they put it on its stand, and it gives light to everyone in the house.

In the same way, let your light shine before men, that they may see your good deeds and praise your Father in heaven.

Matthew 5:14-16

For Christ did not send me to baptize, but to preach the gospel — not with words of human wisdom, lest the cross of Christ be emptied of its power.

For the message of the cross is foolishness to those who are perishing, but to us who are being saved it is the power of God.

For it is written: "I will destroy the wisdom of the wise; the intelligence of the intelligent I will frustrate."

Where is the wise man? Where is the scholar? Where is the philosopher of this age? Has not God made foolish the wisdom of the world?

For since in the wisdom of God the world through its wisdom did not know him, God was pleased through the foolishness of what was preached to save those who believe.

Jews demand miraculous signs and Greeks look for wisdom,

But we preach Christ crucified: a stumbling block to Jews and foolishness to Gentiles,

But to those whom God has called, both Jews and Greeks, Christ the power of God and the wisdom of God.

For the foolishness of God is wiser than man's wisdom, and the weakness of God is stronger than man's strength.

Brothers, think of what you were when you were called. Not many of you were wise by human standards; not many were influential; not many were of noble birth.

But God chose the foolish things of the world to shame the wise; God chose the weak things of the world to shame the strong.

He chose the lowly things of this world and the despised things — and the things that are not — to nullify the things that are,

So that no one may boast before him.
1 Corinthians 1:17-29

When I came to you, brothers, I did not come with eloquence or superior wisdom as I proclaimed to you the testimony about God.

For I resolved to know nothing while I was with you except Jesus Christ and him crucified.

I came to you in weakness and fear, and with much trembling.

My message and my preaching were not with wise and persuasive words, but with a demonstration of the Spirit's power,

So that your faith might not rest on men's wisdom, but on God's power.

1 Corinthians 2:1-5

But thanks be to God, who always leads us in triumphal procession in Christ and through us spreads everywhere the fragrance of the knowledge of him.

2 Corinthians 2:14

To the one we are the smell of death; to the other, the fragrance of life. And who is equal to such a task?

2 Corinthians 2:16

To them God has chosen to make known among the Gentiles the glorious riches of this mystery, which is Christ in you, the hope of glory.

We proclaim him, admonishing and teaching everyone with all wisdom, so that we may present everyone perfect in Christ.

To this end I labor, struggling with all his energy, which so powerfully works in me.

Colossians 1:27-29

Do your best to present yourself to God as one approved, a workman who does not need to be ashamed and who correctly handles the word of truth.

2 Timothy 2:15

So that you may become blameless and pure, children of God without fault in a crooked and depraved generation, in which you shine like stars in the universe.

Philippians 2:15

And teaching them to obey everything I have commanded you. And surely I am with you always, to the very end of the age.

Matthew 28:20

By this all men will know that you are my disciples, if you love one another.

John 13:35

All this is from God, who reconciled us to himself through Christ and gave us the ministry of reconciliation.

2 Corinthians 5:18

But you are a chosen people, a royal priesthood, a holy nation, a people belonging to God, that you may declare the praises of him who called you out of darkness into his wonderful light.

1 Peter 2:9

The Spirit of the Sovereign Lord is on me, because the Lord has anointed me to preach good news to the poor. He has sent me to bind up the brokenhearted, to proclaim freedom for the captives and release from darkness for the prisoners.

Isaiah 61:1

Pray also for me, that whenever I open my mouth, words may be given me so that I will fearlessly make known the mystery of the gospel.

Ephesians 6:19

I am not ashamed of the gospel, because it is the power of God for the salvation of everyone who believes: first for the Jew, then for the Gentile.

For in the gospel a righteousness from God is revealed, a righteousness that is by faith from first to last, just as it is written: "The righteous will live by faith."

Romans 1:16,17

The Bible Promises You Will Win

In him we were also chosen, having been predestined according to the plan of him who works out everything in conformity with the purpose of his will,

In order that we, who were the first to hope in Christ, might be for the praise of his glory.

Ephesians 1:11,12

And afterward, I will pour out my Spirit on all people. Your sons and daughters will prophesy, your old men will dream dreams, your young men will see visions.

Even on my servants, both men and women, I will pour out my Spirit in those days.

Joel 2:28,29

For it is by grace you have been saved, through faith — and this not from yourselves, it is the gift of God —

Not by works, so that no one can boast.

For we are God's workmanship, created in Christ Jesus to do good works, which God prepared in advance for us to do.

Ephesians 2:8-10

Young men and maidens, old men and children.

Let them praise the name of the Lord, for his name alone is exalted; his splendor is above the earth and the heavens.

Psalm 148:12,13

Don't let anyone look down on you because you are young, but set an example for the believers in speech, in life, in love, in faith and in purity.

Until I come, devote yourself to the public reading of Scripture, to preaching and to teaching.

Do not neglect your gift, which was given you through a prophetic message when the body of elders laid their hands on you.

Be diligent in these matters; give yourself wholly to them, so that everyone may see your progress.

Watch your life and doctrine closely. Persevere in them, because if you do, you will save both yourself and your hearers.

1 Timothy 4:12-16

No, this is what was spoken by the prophet Joel:

"In the last days, God says, I will pour out my Spirit on all people. Your sons and daughters will prophesy, your young men will see visions, your old men will dream dreams.

"Even on my servants, both men and women, I will pour out my Spirit in those days, and they will prophesy."

Acts 2:16-18

I will stand at my watch and station myself on the ramparts; I will look to see what he will say to me, and what answer I am to give to this complaint.

Then the Lord replied: "Write down the revelation and make it plain on tablets so that a herald may run with it.

"For the revelation awaits an appointed time; it speaks of the end and will not prove false. Though it linger, wait for it; it will certainly come and will not delay."

Habakkuk 2:1-3

For the earth will be filled with the knowledge of the glory of the Lord, as the waters cover the sea.

Habakkuk 2:14

I write to you, fathers, because you have known him who is from the beginning. I write to you, young men, because you have overcome the evil one. I write to you, dear children, because you have known the Father.

I write to you, fathers, because you have known him who is from the beginning. I write to you, young men, because you are strong, and the word of God lives in you, and you have overcome the evil one.

Do not love the world or anything in the world. If anyone loves the world, the love of the Father is not in him.

For everything in the world — the cravings of sinful man, the lust of his eyes and the boasting of what he has and does — comes not from the Father but from the world.

The world and its desires pass away, but the man who does the will of God lives forever.

1 John 2:13-17

Choosing a Career

I will instruct you and teach you in the way you should go; I will counsel you and watch over you.

Psalm 32:8

Apply your heart to instruction and your ears to words of knowledge.

Proverbs 23:12

Be strong and courageous. Do not be afraid or terrified because of them, for the Lord your

God goes with you; he will never leave you nor forsake you.

Deuteronomy 31:6

You are my lamp, O Lord; the Lord turns my darkness into light.

2 Samuel 22:29

Teach us to number our days aright, that we may gain a heart of wisdom.

Psalm 90:12

Plans fail for lack of counsel, but with many advisers they succeed.

Proverbs 15:22

The purposes of a man's heart are deep waters, but a man of understanding draws them out.

Proverbs 20:5

I will lead the blind by ways they have not known, along unfamiliar paths I will guide them; I will turn the darkness into light before them and make the rough places smooth. These are the things I will do; I will not forsake them.

Isaiah 42:16

Suppose one of you wants to build a tower. Will he not first sit down and estimate the cost to see if he has enough money to complete it?

For if he lays the foundation and is not able to finish it, everyone who sees it will ridicule him,

Saying, "This fellow began to build and was not able to finish."

Luke 14:28-30

Preparing for the Future

Peace I leave with you; my peace I give you. I do not give to you as the world gives. Do not let your hearts be troubled and do not be afraid.

John 14:27

Cast all your anxiety on him because he cares for you.

1 Peter 5:7

He said: "Listen, King Jehoshaphat and all who live in Judah and Jerusalem! This is what the Lord says to you: Do not be afraid or discouraged because of this vast army. For the battle is not yours, but God's."

2 Chronicles 20:15

Do not let this Book of the Law depart from your mouth; meditate on it day and night, so that you may be careful to do everything written in it. Then you will be prosperous and successful.

Joshua 1:8

Commit to the Lord whatever you do, and your plans will succeed.

Proverbs 16:3

Do not be anxious about anything, but in everything, by prayer and petition, with thanksgiving, present your requests to God.

Philippians 4:6

Let us then approach the throne of grace with confidence, so that we may receive mercy and find grace to help us in our time of need.

Hebrews 4:16

So do not throw away your confidence; it will be richly rewarded.

Hebrews 10:35

Looking for Employment

But blessed is the man who trusts in the Lord, whose confidence is in him.

Jeremiah 17:7

This is what the Lord says — your Redeemer, the Holy One of Israel: "I am the Lord your God, who teaches you what is best for you, who directs you in the way you should go."

Isaiah 48:17

And God is able to make all grace abound to you, so that in all things at all times, having all that you need, you will abound in every good work.

2 Corinthians 9:8

Do not be like them, for your Father knows what you need before you ask him.

Matthew 6:8

The Lord himself goes before you and will be with you; he will never leave you nor forsake you. Do not be afraid; do not be discouraged.

Deuteronomy 31:8

Fear of man will prove to be a snare, but whoever trusts in the Lord is kept safe.

Proverbs 29:25

Whether you turn to the right or to the left, your ears will hear a voice behind you, saying, "This is the way; walk in it."

Isaiah 30:21

Look at the birds of the air; they do not sow or reap or store away in barns, and yet your heavenly Father feeds them. Are you not much more valuable than they?

Matthew 6:26

"'If you can'?" said Jesus. "Everything is possible for him who believes."

Mark 9:23

8

SCRIPTURE-BASED PRAYERS

Prayer for Yourself

And pray in the Spirit on all occasions with all kinds of prayers and requests. With this in mind, be alert and always keep on praying for all the saints.

Pray also for me, that whenever I open my mouth, words may be given me so that I will fearlessly make known the mystery of the gospel,

For which I am an ambassador in chains. Pray that I may declare it fearlessly, as I should.

Ephesians 6:18-20

With this in mind, we constantly pray for you, that our God may count you worthy of his calling, and that by his power he may fulfill every good purpose of yours and every act prompted by your faith.

We pray this so that the name of our Lord Jesus may be glorified in you, and you in him, according to the grace of our God and the Lord Jesus Christ.

2 Thessalonians 1:11,12

For this reason I kneel before the Father,

From whom his whole family in heaven and on earth derives its name.

I pray that out of his glorious riches he may strengthen you with power through his Spirit in your inner being,

So that Christ may dwell in your hearts through faith. And I pray that you, being rooted and established in love,

May have power, together with all the saints, to grasp how wide and long and high and deep is the love of Christ,

And to know this love that surpasses knowledge — that you may be filled to the measure of all the fullness of God.

Now to him who is able to do immeasurably more than all we ask or imagine, according to his power that is at work within us,

To him be glory in the church and in Christ Jesus throughout all generations, for ever and ever! Amen.

Ephesians 3:14-21

For this reason, since the day we heard about you, we have not stopped praying for you and asking God to fill you with the knowledge of his will through all spiritual wisdom and understanding.

And we pray this in order that you may live a life worthy of the Lord and may please him in every way: bearing fruit in every good work, growing in the knowledge of God,

Being strengthened with all power according to his glorious might so that you may have great endurance and patience, and joyfully

Giving thanks to the Father, who has qualified you to share in the inheritance of the saints in the kingdom of light.

For he has rescued us from the dominion of darkness and brought us into the kingdom of the Son he loves,

In whom we have redemption, the forgiveness of sins.

Colossians 1:9-14

I keep asking that the God of our Lord Jesus Christ, the glorious Father, may give you the Spirit of wisdom and revelation, so that you may know him better.

I pray also that the eyes of your heart may be enlightened in order that you may know the hope to which he has called you, the riches of his glorious inheritance in the saints,

And his incomparably great power for us who believe. That power is like the working of his mighty strength,

Which he exerted in Christ when he raised him from the dead and seated him at his right hand in the heavenly realms,

Far above all rule and authority, power and dominion, and every title that can be given, not only in the present age but also in the one to come.

And God placed all things under his feet and appointed him to be head over everything for the church,

Which is his body, the fullness of him who fills everything in every way.

Ephesians 1:17-23

And this is my prayer: That your love may abound more and more in knowledge and depth of insight,

So that you may be able to discern what is best and may be pure and blameless until the day of Christ,

Filled with the fruit of righteousness that comes through Jesus Christ — to the glory and praise of God.

Philippians 1:9-11

To Timothy my true son in the faith: Grace, mercy and peace from God the Father and Christ Jesus our Lord.

As I urged you when I went into Macedonia, stay there in Ephesus so that you may command certain men not to teach false doctrines any longer

Nor to devote themselves to myths and endless genealogies. These promote controversies rather than God's work — which is by faith.

The goal of this command is love, which comes from a pure heart and a good conscience and a sincere faith.

Some have wandered away from these and turned to meaningless talk.

1 Timothy 1:2-6

Making God's Word a Priority in Your Life

Your word is a lamp to my feet and a light for my path.

Psalm 119:105

Do not let this Book of the Law depart from your mouth; meditate on it day and night, so that you may be careful to do everything written in it. Then you will be prosperous and successful.

Joshua 1:8

Do not merely listen to the word, and so deceive yourselves. Do what it says.

James 1:22

For everything that was written in the past was written to teach us, so that through endurance and the encouragement of the Scriptures we might have hope.

Romans 15:4

All Scripture is God-breathed and is useful for teaching, rebuking, correcting and training in righteousness.

2 Timothy 3:16

Heaven and earth will pass away, but my words will never pass away.

Mark 13:31

Jesus answered, "It is written: 'Man does not live on bread alone, but on every word that comes from the mouth of God.'"

Matthew 4:4

For the word of God is living and active. Sharper than any double-edged sword, it penetrates even to dividing soul and spirit, joints and marrow; it judges the thoughts and attitudes of the heart.

Hebrews 4:12

For prophecy never had its origin in the will of man, but men spoke from God as they were carried along by the Holy Spirit.

2 Peter 1:21

But his delight is in the law of the Lord, and on his law he meditates day and night.

Psalm 1:2

I am sending him to you for the express purpose that you may know about our circumstances and that he may encourage your hearts.

Colossians 4:8

He sent forth his word and healed them; he rescued them from the grave.

Psalm 107:20

Like newborn babies, crave pure spiritual milk, so that by it you may grow up in your salvation.

1 Peter 2:2

To the Jews who had believed him, Jesus said, "If you hold to my teaching, you are really my disciples.

"Then you will know the truth, and the truth will set you free."

John 8:31,32

Consequently, faith comes from hearing the message, and the message is heard through the word of Christ.

Romans 10:17

But the word of the Lord stands forever. And this is the word that was preached to you.

1 Peter 1:25

He remembers his covenant forever, the word he commanded, for a thousand generations.

1 Chronicles 16:15

In God, whose word I praise, in God I trust; I will not be afraid. What can mortal man do to me?

Psalm 56:4

Jesus, who is called Justus, also sends greetings. These are the only Jews among my fellow workers for the kingdom of God, and they have proved a comfort to me.

Colossians 4:11

Making Prayer a Priority in Your Life

And I will do whatever you ask in my name, so that the Son may bring glory to the Father.

You may ask me for anything in my name, and I will do it.

John 14:13,14

Do not be anxious about anything, but in everything, by prayer and petition, with thanksgiving, present your requests to God.

Philippians 4:6

I tell you the truth, if anyone says to this mountain, "Go, throw yourself into the sea," and does not doubt in his heart but believes that what he says will happen, it will be done for him.

Therefore I tell you, whatever you ask for in prayer, believe that you have received it, and it will be yours.

Mark 11:23,24

Therefore confess your sins to each other and pray for each other so that you may be healed. The prayer of a righteous man is powerful and effective.

James 5:16

If my people, who are called by my name, will humble themselves and pray and seek my face and turn from their wicked ways, then will I hear from heaven and will forgive their sin and will heal their land.

2 Chronicles 7:14

My heart says of you, "Seek his face!" Your face, Lord, I will seek.

Psalm 27:8

Ask and it will be given to you; seek and you will find; knock and the door will be opened to you.

For everyone who asks receives; he who seeks finds; and to him who knocks, the door will be opened.

Matthew 7:7,8

If you remain in me and my words remain in you, ask whatever you wish, and it will be given you.

John 15:7

In that day you will no longer ask me anything. I tell you the truth, my Father will give you whatever you ask in my name.

Until now you have not asked for anything in my name. Ask and you will receive, and your joy will be complete.

John 16:23,24

But you, dear friends, build yourselves up in your most holy faith and pray in the Holy Spirit.

Jude 20

This is the confidence we have in approaching God: that if we ask anything according to his will, he hears us.

And if we know that he hears us — whatever we ask — we know that we have what we asked of him.

1 John 5:14,15

Let us then approach the throne of grace with confidence, so that we may receive mercy and find grace to help us in our time of need.

Hebrews 4:16

The eyes of the Lord are on the righteous and his ears are attentive to their cry.

Psalm 34:15

Call to me and I will answer you and tell you great and unsearchable things you do not know.

Jeremiah 33:3

Again, I tell you that if two of you on earth agree about anything you ask for, it will be done for you by my Father in heaven.

Matthew 18:19

If you believe, you will receive whatever you ask for in prayer.

Matthew 21:22

P<small>ART III</small>
31-D<small>AY</small>

DEVOTIONAL

by
John Mason

D~AY~ 1

YOUR LEAST FAVORITE COLOR
SHOULD BE BEIGE.

Never try to defend your present position and situation. Choose to be a person who is on the offensive, not the defensive. **People who live defensively never rise above being average.** We're called, as Christians, to be on the offensive, to take the initiative. A lukewarm, indecisive person is never secure regardless of his wealth, education, or position.

Don't ever let your quest for balance become an excuse for not taking the unique, radical, invading move that God has directed you to take. Many times the attempt to maintain balance in life is really just an excuse for being lukewarm. In Joshua 1:6,7,9 the Lord says three times to Joshua, "Be strong and courageous." I believe that He is saying the same thing to all believers today.

When you choose to be on the offensive, the atmosphere of your life will begin to change. So if you don't like the atmosphere of your life, choose to take the offensive position. Taking the offensive is not just an action taken outside a person; it is always a decision made within.

When you do choose to be on the offensive, keep all your conflicts impersonal. Fight the issue, not the person. Speak about what God in you can do, not what others cannot do. **You will find that when all of your reasons are defensive, your cause almost never succeeds.**

Being on the offensive and taking the initiative is a master key which opens the door to opportunity in your life. Learn to create a habit of taking the initiative and **don't ever start your day in neutral**. Every morning when your feet hit the floor, you should be thinking on the offensive, reacting like an invader, taking control of your day and your life.

By pulling back and being defensive usually you enhance the problem. Intimidation always precedes defeat. If you are not sure which way to go, pray and move towards the situation in confident trust.

Be like the two fishermen who got trapped in a storm in the middle of the lake. One turned to the other and asked, "Should we pray, or should we row?" His wise companion responded, "Let's do both!"

That's taking the offensive.

D_{AY} 2

GROWTH COMES FROM BUILDING ON TALENTS, GIFTS, AND STRENGTHS — NOT BY SOLVING PROBLEMS.

One of the most neglected areas in many people's lives is the area of gifts that God has placed within them. It is amazing how some people can devote their entire lives to a field of endeavor or a profession that has nothing to do with their inborn talents. In fact, the opposite is also true. Many people spend their whole lifetime trying to change who God has made them to be. They ignore their God-given talents while continually seeking to change their natural makeup. As children of God, we need to recognize our innate gifts, talents, and strengths and do everything in our power to build on them.

One good thing about God's gifts and calling is that they are permanent and enduring. Romans 11:29 tells us: *...the gifts and calling of God are without repentance.* The Greek word translated *repentance* in this verse means "irrevocable." God cannot take away His gifts and calling in your life. **Even if you've never done anything with them, even if you've failed time and time again, God's gifts and calling are still resident**

within you. They are there this day, and you can choose to do something with them, beginning right now.

Gifts and talents are really God's deposits in our personal accounts, but we determine the interest on them. The greater the amount of interest and attention we give to them, the greater their value becomes. **God's gifts are never loans; they are always deposits.** As such, they are never used up or depleted. In fact, the more they are used, the greater, stronger, and more valuable they become. When they are put to good use, they provide information, insight, and revelation which cannot be received any other way or from any other source.

As Christians, we need to make full use of all the gifts and talents which God has bestowed upon us so that we do not abound in one area while becoming bankrupt in another. Someone has said, "If the only tool you have is a hammer, you tend to treat everything like a nail." Don't make that mistake; use all of the gifts God has given you. If you choose not to step out and make maximum use of the gifts and talents in your life, you will spend your days on this earth helping someone else reach his goals. Most people let others control their destiny. Don't allow anyone to take over the driver's seat in your life. Fulfill your own dreams and determine your own life's course.

Never underestimate the power of the gifts that are within you. **Gifts and talents are given** us to use not only so we can fulfill to the fullest the call in our own lives, but also so we can reach the souls who are attached to those gifts. There are people whose lives are waiting to be affected by what God has placed within you. So evaluate yourself. Define and refine your gifts, talents and strengths. Choose today to look for opportunities to exercise your unique God-endowed, God-ordained gifts and calling.

DAY 3

"THE NOSE OF THE BULLDOG IS SLANTED BACKWARDS SO HE CAN CONTINUE TO BREATHE WITHOUT LETTING GO." — WINSTON CHURCHILL

Persistent people begin their success where most others quit. We Christians need to be known as people of persistence and endurance. **One person with commitment, persistence, and endurance will accomplish more than a thousand people with interest alone.** In Hebrews 12:1 (NIV) we read: *Therefore, since we are surrounded by such a great cloud of witnesses, let us throw off everything that hinders and the sin that so easily entangles, and let us run with perseverance the race marked out for us.* The more diligently we work, the harder it is to quit. Persistence is a habit; so is quitting.

Never worry about how much money, ability, or equipment you are starting with. Just begin with a million dollars worth of determination. Remember: **it's not what you have, it's what you do with what you have that makes all the difference**. Many people eagerly begin "the good fight of faith," but they forget to add patience, persistence, and endurance to their enthusiasm. Josh Billings said, "Consider the postage stamp. Its usefulness consists in the ability to stick to something until it gets there." You and I should be known as "postage-stamp" Christians.

In First Corinthians 15:58, the Apostle Paul writes: *Therefore, my beloved brethren, be ye stedfast, unmoveable, always abounding in the work of the Lord, forasmuch as ye know that your labour is not in vain in the Lord.* Peter tells us: *Wherefore, beloved, seeing that ye look for such things, be diligent that ye may be found of him in peace, without spot, and blameless* (2 Pet. 3:14). And wise Solomon points out: *Seest thou a man diligent in his business? he shall stand before kings...*(Prov. 22:29).

In the Far East the people plant a tree called the Chinese bamboo. During the first four years they water and fertilize the plant with seemingly little or no results. Then the fifth year they again apply water and fertilizer — and in five weeks' time the tree grows ninety feet in height! The obvious question is: did the Chinese bamboo tree grow ninety feet in five weeks, or did it grow ninety feet in five years? The answer is: it grew ninety feet in five years. Because if at any time during those five years the people had stopped watering and fertilizing the tree, it would have died.

Many times our dreams and plans appear not to be succeeding. We are tempted to give up and quit trying. Instead, we need to continue to water and fertilize those dreams and plans, nurturing the seeds of the vision God has placed within us. Because we know that if we do not quit, if we display perseverance and endurance, we will also reap a harvest. Charles Haddon Spurgeon said, "By perseverance the snail reached the ark." We need to be like that snail.

D~AY~ 4

**WE CAN GROW BY OUR QUESTIONS, AS
WELL AS BY OUR ANSWERS.**

Here are some important questions we
should ask ourselves:

1. What one decision would I make if I
    knew that it would not fail?

2. What one thing should I eliminate from
    my life because it holds me back from
    reaching my full potential?

3. Am I on the path of something ab-
    solutely marvelous, or something ab-
    solutely mediocre?

4. If everyone in the United States of
    America were on my level of spirituality,
    would there be a revival in the land?

5. Does the devil know who I am?

6. Am I running from something, or to
    something?

7. What can I do to make better use of my
    time?

8. Would I recognize Jesus if I met Him on
    the street?

9. Who do I need to forgive?

10. What is my favorite scripture for myself,
    my family, my career?

11. What impossible thing am I believing and planning for?

12. What is my most prevailing thought?

13. What good thing have I previously committed myself to do that I have quit doing?

14. Of the people I respect most, what is it about them that earns my respect?

15. What would a truly creative person do in my situation?

16. What outside influences are causing me to be better or worse?

17. Can I lead anyone else to Christ?

18. In what areas do I need improvement in terms of personal development?

19. What gifts, talents, or strengths do I have?

20. What is one thing that I can do for someone else who has no opportunity to repay me?

D_AY 5

DON'T ASK TIME WHERE IT'S GONE; TELL IT WHERE TO GO.

All great achievers, all successful people, are those who have been able to gain control over their time. It has been said that all human beings have been created equal in one respect: each person has been given 24 hours each day.

We need to choose to give our best time to our most challenging situation. It's not how much we do that matters; it's how much we get done. We should choose to watch our time, not our watch. One of the best timesavers is the ability to say no. Not saying no when you should is one of the biggest wastes of time you will ever experience.

Don't spend a dollar's worth of time for ten cents' worth of results.

Make sure to take care of the vulnerable times in your days. These vulnerable times are the first thing in the morning and the last thing at night. I have heard a minister say that what a person is like at midnight when he is all alone reveals that person's true self.

Never allow yourself to say, "I could be doing big things if I weren't so busy doing small things!" Take control of your time. **The greater control you exercise over your time, the greater**

freedom you will experience in your life. The psalmist prayed, *So teach us to number our days, that we may apply our hearts unto wisdom* (Ps. 90:12). The Bible teaches us that the devil comes to steal, and to kill, and to destroy (John 10:10), and this verse applies to time as well as to people. The enemy desires to provide God's children with ideas of how to kill, steal, and destroy valuable time.

People are always saying, "I'd give anything to be able to. . ." There is a basic leadership principle that says, "6 x 1 = 6." If you want to write a book, learn to play a musical instrument, become a better tennis player, or do anything else important, then you should devote one hour a day, six days a week, to the project. Sooner than you think, what you desire will become reality. There are not many things that a person cannot accomplish in 312 hours a year! Just a commitment of one hour a day, six days a week, is all it takes.

We all have the same amount of time each day. The difference between people is determined by what they do with the amount of time at their disposal. Don't be like the airline pilot flying over the Pacific Ocean who reported to his passengers, "We're lost, but we're making great time!" Remember that the future arrives an hour at a time. **Gain control of your time, and you will gain control of your life.**

D<small>AY</small> 6

DON'T CONSUME YOUR TOMORROWS FEEDING ON YOUR YESTERDAYS.

Decide today to get rid of any "loser's limps" which you may still be carrying from some past experience. As followers of Jesus Christ, you and I need to break the power of the past to dominate our present and determine our future.

In Luke 9:62, Jesus said, ...*No man, having put his hand to the plough, and looking back, is fit for the kingdom of God*. If we are not careful, we will allow the past to exercise a great hold on us. **The more we look backward, the less able we are to see forward.** The past makes no difference concerning what God can do for us today.

That is the beauty of the Christian life. Even when we have failed, we are able to ask for forgiveness and be totally cleansed of and released from our past actions. Whatever hold the past may have on us can be broken. It is never God who holds us back. It is always our own choosing to allow the past to keep us from living to the fullest in the present and future. Failure is waiting around the corner for those who are living off of yesterday's successes and failures. **We should choose to be forward-**

focused, not past-possessed. We should learn to profit from the past, but to invest in the future.

In Philippians 3:13,14, the Apostle Paul writes:

Brethren, I count not myself to have apprehended: but this one thing I do, forgetting those things which are behind, and reaching forth unto those things which are before,

I press toward the mark for the prize of the high calling of God in Christ Jesus.

The key here is "forgetting those things which are behind" in order to reach for "the high calling of God in Christ Jesus." To fulfill our calling in Christ, we must first forget that which lies behind. Probably the most common stronghold in a person's life is his past mistakes and failures. Today is the day to begin to shake off the shackles of the past and move forward.

The past is past. It has no life.

D~AY~ 7

THE BEST TIME OF DAY IS NOW.

Procrastination is a killer.

When you choose to kill time, you begin to kill those gifts and callings which God has placed within your life. *The Living Bible* paraphrase of Ecclesiastes 11:4 reads: *If you wait for perfect conditions, you will never get anything done.*

The first step in overcoming procrastination is to eliminate all excuses and reasons for not taking decisive and immediate action.

Everybody is on the move. They are moving forwards, backwards, or on a treadmill. The mistake most people make is thinking that the main goal of life is to stay busy. Such thinking is a trap. What is important is not whether a person is busy, but whether he is progressing. It is a question of activity versus accomplishment.

A gentleman named John Henry Fabre conducted an experiment with processionary caterpillars. They are so named because of their peculiar habit of blindly following each other no matter how they are lined up or where they are going. This man took a group of these tiny creatures and did something interesting with them. He placed them in a circle. For 24 hours the caterpillars dutifully followed one another around and around. Then he did something else. He placed the caterpillars around a saucer full of pine needles (their favorite food). For six days the mindless creatures moved around and around the saucer, literally dying from starvation and exhaustion even though an abundance of choice food was located less than two inches away.

You see, they had confused activity with accomplishment.

We Christians need to be known as those who accomplish great things for God — not those who simply talk about it. Procrastinators are good at talking versus doing. It is true what Mark Twain said: "Noise produces nothing. Often a hen who has merely laid an egg cackles as though she has laid an asteroid."

We need to be like the apostles. They were never known much for their policies or procedures, their theories or excuses. Instead, they were known for their acts. Many people say that they are waiting for God; but in most cases God is waiting for them. We need to say with the psalmist, "Lord, my times are in Your hands." (Ps. 31:15.) The price of growth is always less than the cost of stagnation. As Edmund Burke said, "The only thing necessary for the triumph of evil is for good men to do nothing."

Occasionally you may see someone who doesn't do anything, and yet seems to be successful in life. Don't be deceived. The old saying is true: "Even a broken clock is right twice a day." As Christians we are called to make progress — not excuses.

Procrastination is a primary tool of the devil to hold us back and to make us miss God's timing in our lives. *The desire of the slothful killeth him; for his hands refuse to labour* (Prov. 21:25). **The fact is, the longer we take to act on God's direction, the more unclear it becomes.**

D<small>AY</small> 8

FEAR AND WORRY ARE INTEREST PAID IN ADVANCE ON SOMETHING YOU MAY NEVER OWN.

Fear is a poor chisel to carve out tomorrow. Worry is simply the triumph of fear over faith.

There's a story that is told about a woman who was standing on a street corner crying profusely. A man came up to her and asked why she was weeping. The lady shook her head and replied: "I was just thinking that maybe someday I would get married. We would later have a beautiful baby girl. Then one day this child and I would go for a walk along this street, come to this corner, and my darling daughter would run into the street, get hit by a car, and die."

Now that sounds like a pretty ridiculous situation — for a grown woman to be weeping her eyes out because of something that would probably never happen. Yet isn't this the way we respond when we worry? We take a situation or event which might never exist and build it up all out of proportion in our mind.

There is an old Swedish proverb that says, "Worry gives a small thing a big shadow." **Worry is simply the misuse of God's creative**

imagination which He has placed within each of us. When fear rises in our mind, we should learn to expect the opposite in our life.

The word *worry* itself is derived from an Anglo-Saxon term meaning "to strangle," or "to choke off." There is no question that worry and fear in the mind does choke off the creative flow from above.

Things are seldom as they seem. "Skim milk masquerades as cream," said W.S. Gilbert. As we dwell on and worry about matters beyond our control, a negative effect begins to set in. Too much analysis always leads to paralysis. *Worry is a route which leads from somewhere to nowhere. Don't let it direct your life.*

In Psalm 55:22 the Bible says, *Cast thy burden upon the Lord, and he shall sustain thee: he shall never suffer the righteous to be moved.* Never respond out of fear, and never fear to respond. Action attacks fear; inaction builds fear.

Don't worry and don't fear. Instead, take your fear and worry to the Lord, *Casting all your care upon him; for he careth for you* (1 Pet. 5:7).

D<small>AY</small> 9

OUR WORDS ARE SEEDS PLANTED INTO OTHER PEOPLE'S LIVES.

What we say is important. The Bible states that out of the abundance of the heart the mouth speaks. (Matt. 12:34.) We need to change our vocabulary. We need to speak words of life and light. Our talk should always rise to the level of the Word of God.

We Christians should be known as people who speak positively, those who speak the Word of God into situations, those who speak forth words of life.

We should not be like the man who joined a monastery in which the monks were allowed to speak only two words every seven years. After the first seven years had passed, the new initiate met with the abbot who asked him, "Well, what are your two words?"

"Food's bad," replied the man, who then went back to spend another seven-year period before once again meeting with his ecclesiastical superior.

"What are your two words now?" asked the clergyman.

"Bed's hard," responded the man.

Seven years later — twenty-one years after his initial entry into the monastery — the man met with the abbot for the third and final time.

"And what are your two words this time?" he was asked.

"I quit."

"Well, I'm not surprised," answered the disgusted cleric, "all you've done since you got here is complain!"

Don't be like that man; don't be known as a person whose only words are negative.

If you are a member of the "murmuring grapevine," you need to resign. In John 6:43 our Lord instructed His disciples, ...*Murmur not among yourselves*. In Philippians 2:14,15 the Apostle Paul exhorted the believers of his day:

Do all things without murmurings and disputings:

That ye may be blameless and harmless, the sons of God, without rebuke, in the midst of a crooked and perverse nation, among whom ye shine as lights in the world.

Contrary to what you may have heard, talk is not cheap. Talk is very expensive. We should know that our words are powerful. What we say affects what we get from others, and what others get from us. When we speak the wrong word, it lessens our ability to see and hear the will of God.

D<small>AY</small> 10

VERSUS.

Every day we make decisions. Daily we are confronted with options. **We must choose one or the other.** We cannot have both. These options include:

Being bitter versus being better.

Indifference versus decisiveness.

Lukewarmness versus enthusiasm.

"If we can" versus "how we can."

"Give up" versus "get up."

Security versus risk.

Coping with evil versus overcoming evil.

Blending in versus standing out.

How much we do versus how much we get done.

Coexisting with darkness versus opposing darkness.

Destruction versus development.

Resisting versus receiving.

Complaining versus obtaining.

Trying versus committing.

Peace versus strife.

Choice versus chance.

Determination versus discouragement.

Growing versus dying.

Demanding more of ourselves versus excusing ourselves.

Doing for others versus doing for self.

Progress versus regression.

Steering versus drifting.

Priorities versus aimlessness.

Accountability versus irresponsibility.

Action versus activity.

Solutions versus problems.

More of God versus more of everything else.

Being in "Who's Who" versus asking "Why me?"

D<small>AY</small> 11

KEEP YOUR FEET ON THE ROCK WHEN YOU REACH THE END OF YOUR ROPE.

Don't quit. There is a big difference between quitting and changing. I believe that **when God sees someone who doesn't quit, He looks down and says, "There is someone I can use."**

In Galatians 6:9 (NIV) we are told, *Let us not become weary in doing good, for at the proper time we will reap a harvest if we do not give up.* Look at this verse carefully. It urges us not to become weary, assuring us that we will — not might — reap a harvest if we do not give up.

God doesn't quit. It is impossible for Him to do so. In Philippians 1:6 (NIV) the Apostle Paul writes about *being confident of this, that he who began a good work in you will carry it on to completion until the day of Christ Jesus.* There are several important points in this verse. The most crucial is the fact that God does not quit. Therefore, we can have great confidence that He will complete the good work He has begun in us. He will see us through every step of the way until we have reached our ultimate destination.

One of the best scriptural examples of a person who did not quit is Joseph. He had many reasons to justify giving up. First, when he was trapped in the pit into which his brothers had thrown him because of their jealousy, I am sure he said to himself, "This is not the way I dreamed my life would work out." Later on, he had a marvelous opportunity to become discouraged and quit when he was unjustly accused and thrown into prison for a crime he did not commit. Again he could have said to himself, "This is not right; I'm not supposed to be here."

But eventually the dream which God had given Joseph became reality. He was elevated from prisoner to prime minister in one day. Although Joseph did not know or understand the steps through which the Lord would lead him, he remained true to his God. Despite the trials and obstacles he faced, he did not quit.

There is no greater reward than that which comes as a result of holding fast to the Word and will of God. Only you can decide not to lose. Most people quit right on the verge of success. Often it is right at their fingertips. There is only one degree of difference between hot water and steam.

In Luke 18 (NIV) Jesus told the parable of the persistent widow. The Bible reveals His purpose in relating this story: *Then Jesus told his disciples a parable to show them they should always pray and not give up* (v. 1). The psalmist tells us, *Commit thy way unto the Lord; trust also in him; and he shall bring it to pass* (Ps. 37:5).

The only way we can lose is to quit. That is the only decision we can make that can keep us from reaching God's goals in our lives.

D<small>AY</small> 12

A GOAL IS A DREAM WITH A DEADLINE.

In Habakkuk 2:2 the Lord tells the prophet, *...Write the vision, and make it plain upon tables, that he may run that readeth it*. The key to successful goal-setting is revealed in this scripture.

First, the vision must be written down. When you keep a vision in your mind, it is not really a goal; it is really nothing more than a dream. There is power in putting that dream down on paper. When you commit something to writing, commitment to achievement naturally follows. You can't start a fire with paper alone, but writing something down on paper can start a fire inside of you.

God Himself followed His Word here, by taking His vision for us and having it put down on paper in the form of the Bible. He did not just rely on the Holy Spirit to guide and direct us; He put His goals down in writing. We are told to make the word of the Lord plain upon "tables" (tablets) so that it is clear and specific as to what the vision is "...so that he may run that readeth it."

The key word is "run." God desires that we run with the vision and goal in our life. As long as we are running with the vision, we won't turn around. When you walk with a vision, it's easy to change directions and go the wrong way. **You can't stroll to a goal.**

In Proverbs 24:3,4 (TLB), we read: *Any enterprise is built by wise planning, becomes strong through common sense, and profits wonderfully by keeping abreast of the facts*. Simply stated, effective goal-setting and planning provides an opportunity to bring the future to the present and deal with it today. You will find that achievement is easy when your outer goals become an inner commitment.

Even though we have the Holy Spirit, we still need to prepare; we are just better equipped to do so. God's first choice for us in any situation cannot be disorder and waste of funds or resources. That's why proper planning is so important. Plan to the potential. Believe for God's biggest dream. When you plan, look to the future, not the past. You can't drive forward by looking out the rear window.

Always involve yourself with something that's bigger than you are, because that's where God is. Every great success was, at the beginning, impossible. We all have opportunity for success in our lives. It takes just as much energy and effort for a bad life as it does for a good life; yet most people live meaningless lives simply because they never decided to write their vision down and then follow through on it. Know this, if you can't see the mark, you can't press towards it.

Ponder the path of thy feet, and let all thy ways be established (Prov. 4:26). You will find that what you learn on the path to your goals is actually more valuable than achieving the goal itself. Columbus discovered America while searching for a route to India. Be on the lookout for the "Americas" in your path. Put God's vision for your life on paper, and begin to run with His plan.

DAY 13

SMILE — IT ADDS TO YOUR FACE VALUE.

Christians should be the happiest, most enthusiastic, people on earth. In fact, the word *enthusiasm* comes from a Greek word, *entheous* which means "God within" or "full of God."

Smiling — being happy and enthusiastic — is always a choice and not a result. It is a decision that must be consciously made. Enthusiasm and joy and happiness will improve your personality and people's opinion of you. It will help you keep a proper perspective on life. Helen Keller said, "Keep your face to the sunshine and you cannot see the shadow."

The bigger the challenge you are facing, the more enthusiasm you need. Philippians 2:5 (NIV) says, *Your attitude should be the same as that of Christ Jesus.* I believe Jesus was a man Who had a smile on His face, a spring in His step, and joy on His countenance.

Our attitude always tells others what we expect in return.

A smile is a powerful weapon. It can even break the ice. You'll find that being happy and enthusiastic is like a head cold — it's very, very contagious. A laugh a day will keep negative people away. You will also find that as enthusiasm increases, stress and fear in your life will decrease. The Bible says that the joy of the Lord is our strength. (Neh. 8:10.)

Many people say, "Well, no wonder that person is happy, confident, and positive; if I had his job and assets, I would be too." Such thinking falsely assumes that successful people are positive because they have a good income and lots of possessions. But the reverse is true. Such people probably have a good income and lots of possessions as a result of being positive, confident, and happy.

Enthusiasm always motivates to action. No significant accomplishment has ever been made without enthusiasm. In John 15:10,11 (NIV) we have a promise from the Lord, *"If you obey my commands, you will remain in my love, just as I have obeyed my Father's commands and remain in his love. I have told you this so that my joy may be in you and that your joy may be complete."*

The joy and love of the Lord are yours — so smile!

DAY 14

DON'T QUIT AFTER A VICTORY.

There are two times when a person stops: after a defeat and after a victory. Eliminating this kind of procrastination increases momentum.

Robert Schuller has a good saying: "Don't cash in, cast into deeper water." Don't stop after a success, keep the forward momentum going.

One of the great prizes of victory is the opportunity to do more. The trouble is, we've innoculated ourselves with small doses of success which keep us from catching the real thing.

As I was writing this section on momentum, I couldn't get out of my mind a picture of a large boulder at the top of a hill. This boulder represents our lives. If we rock the boulder back and forth and get it moving, its momentum will make it almost unstoppable. The same is true of us.

The Bible promises us God's divine momentum in our lives. In Philippians 1:6 the Apostle Paul writes, *Being confident of this very thing, that he which hath begun a good work in you will perform it until the day of Jesus Christ.* God's momentum always results in growth.

There are five ways to have divine momentum in your life:

1. Be fruitful. (2 Cor. 9:10.)

2. Speak the truth. (Eph. 4:15.)

3. Be spiritually mature. (Heb. 6:1.)

4. Crave the Word of God. (1 Pet. 2:2.)

5. Grow in the grace and knowledge of Jesus. (2 Pet. 3:18.)

God's definition of spiritual momentum is found in 2 Peter 1:5 (NIV):

For this very reason, make every effort to add to your faith goodness; and to goodness, knowledge; and to knowledge, self-control; and to self-control, perseverance; and to perseverance, godliness; and to godliness, brotherly kindness; and to brotherly kindness, love. For if you possess these qualities in increasing measure, they will keep you from being ineffective and unproductive in your knowledge of our Lord Jesus Christ.

Let go of whatever makes you stop.

D~AY~ 15

THE MOST NATURAL THING TO DO
WHEN YOU GET KNOCKED DOWN
IS TO GET UP.

How we respond to failure and mistakes is one of the most important decisions we make every day. Failure doesn't mean that nothing has been accomplished. There is always the opportunity to learn something. What is in you will always be bigger than whatever is around you.

We all experience failure and make mistakes. In fact, successful people always have more failure in their lives than average people do. You will find that throughout history all great people, at some point in their lives, have failed. **Only those who do not expect anything are never disappointed. Only those who never try, never fail.** Anyone who is currently achieving anything in life is simultaneously risking failure. It is always better to fail in doing something than to excel in doing nothing. A flawed diamond is more valuable than a perfect brick. People who have no failures also have few victories.

Everybody gets knocked down, it's how fast he gets up that counts. There is a positive correlation between spiritual maturity and how quickly a person responds to his failures and mistakes. The greater the degree of spiritual maturity, the greater the ability to get back up and go on. The less the spiritual maturity, the longer the individual will continue to hang on to past failures. Every person knows someone who, to this day, is still held back by mistakes he made years ago. God never sees any of us as failures; He only sees us as learners.

We have only failed when we do not learn from the experience. The decision is up to us. We can choose to turn a failure into a hitching post, or a guidepost.

Here is the key to being free from the stranglehold of past failures and mistakes: learn the lesson and forget the details. Gain from the experience, but do not roll over and over in your mind the minute details of it. Build on the experience, and get on with your life.

Remember: **the call is higher than the fall.**

Day 16

THOSE WHO DON'T TAKE CHANCES DON'T MAKE ADVANCES.

All great discoveries have been made by people whose faith ran ahead of their minds. Significant achievements have not been obtained by taking small risks on unimportant issues. Don't ever waste time planning, analyzing, and risking on small ideas. It is always wise to spend more time on decisions that are irreversible and less time on those that are reversible.

Learn to stretch, to reach out where God is. Aim high and take risks. The world's approach is to look to next year based on last year. We Christians need to reach to the potential, not reckon to the past. Those who make great strides are those who take chances and plan toward the challenges of life.

Don't become so caught up in small matters that you can't take advantage of important opportunities. Most people spend their entire lives letting down buckets into empty wells. They continue to waste away their days trying to draw them up again.

Choose today to dream big, to strive to reach the full potential of your calling. Choose to major on the important issues of life, not on the unimportant. H. Stern said, "If you're hunting rabbits in tiger country, you must keep your eye peeled for tigers, but when you are hunting tigers you can ignore the rabbits." There are plenty of tigers to go around. Don't be distracted by or seek after the rabbits of life. Set your sights on "big game."

Security and opportunity are total strangers. If an undertaking doesn't include faith, it's not worthy of being called God's direction. I don't believe that God would call any of us to do anything that would not include an element of faith in Him.

There is a famous old saying that goes, "Even a turtle doesn't get ahead unless he sticks his neck out." **Dream big, because you serve a big God.**

D<small>AY</small> 17

YOUR BEST FRIENDS ARE THOSE WHO BRING OUT THE BEST IN YOU.

We need to be careful of the kind of insulation we use in our lives. We need to insulate ourselves from negative people and ideas. But, we should never insulate ourselves from godly counsel and wisdom.

It is a fact that misery wants your company. In Proverbs 27:19 (TLB) we read, *A mirror reflects a man's face, but what he is really like is shown by the kind of friends he chooses*. Proverbs 13:20 tells us, *He that walketh with wise men shall be wise: but a companion of fools shall be destroyed*. We become like those with whom we associate.

Some years ago I found myself at a stagnation point in my life. I was unproductive and unable to see clearly God's direction. One day I noticed that almost all of my friends were in the same situation. When we got together, all we talked about was our problems. As I prayed about this matter, God showed me that He desired that I have "foundational-level" people in my life. Such people who bring out the best in us, those who influence us to become better people ourselves. They cause us to have greater faith and confidence, to see things from God's perspective. After being with them, our spirits and our sights are raised.

I have found that **it is better to be alone than in the wrong company**. A single conversation with the right person can be more valuable than many years of study.

The Lord showed me that I needed to change my closest associations, and that there were some other people I needed to have contact with on a regular basis. These were men and women of great faith, those who made me a better person just by being around them. They were the ones who saw the gifts in me and could correct me in a constructive, loving way. My choice to change my closest associations was a turning point in my life.

When you surround yourself and affiliate with the right kind of people, you enter into the God-ordained power of agreement. Ecclesiastes 4:9,10,12 (TLB) states:

Two can accomplish more than twice as much as one, for the results can be much better. If one falls, the other pulls him up; but if a man falls when he is alone, he's in trouble.

And one standing alone can be attacked and defeated, but two can stand back-to-back and conquer; three is even better, for a triple-braided cord is not easily broken.

You need to steer clear of negative-thinking "experts." **Remember: in the eyes of average**

people average is always considered out-standing. Look carefully at the closest associations in your life, for that is the direction you are heading.

DAY 18

WE ARE CALLED TO STAND OUT, NOT BLEND IN.

A majority, many times, is a group of highly motivated snails. If a thousand people say something foolish, it's still foolish. Truth is never dependent upon consensus of opinion.

In 1 Peter 2:9, the Bible says of us Christians, *...ye are a chosen generation, a royal priesthood, an holy nation, a peculiar people; that ye should shew forth the praises of him who hath called you out of darkness into his marvellous light.*

Romans 12:2 exhorts us, *And be not conformed to this world, but be ye transformed by the renewing of your mind, that ye may prove what is that good, and acceptable, and perfect, will of God.*

One of the greatest compliments that anybody can give you is to say that you are different. We Christians live in this world, but we are aliens. We should talk differently, act differently, and perform differently. We are called to stand out.

There should be something different about you. If you don't stand out in a group, if there is not something unique or different in your life, you should re-evaluate yourself.

One way to stand head and shoulders above the crowd is to choose to do regular, ordinary things in an extraordinary and supernatural way with great enthusiasm. God has always done some of His very best work through remnants, when the circumstances appear to be stacked against them. In fact, in every battle described in the Bible, God was always on the side of the "underdog," the minority.

Majority rule is not always right. It is usually those people who don't have dreams or visions of their own who want to take a vote. People in groups tend to agree on courses of action that they as individuals know are not right.

Don't be persuaded or dissuaded by group opinion. It doesn't make any difference whether anyone else believes, you must believe. **Never take direction from a crowd for your personal life. And never choose to quit just because somebody else disagrees with you.** In fact, the two worst things you can say to yourself when you get an idea is: 1) "That has never been done before," and 2) "That has been done before." Just because somebody else has gone a particular way and not succeeded does not mean that you too will fail.

Be a pioneer, catch a few arrows, and stand out.

Day 19

SAY NO TO MANY GOOD IDEAS.

One of the tricks of the devil is to get us to say yes to too many things. Then we end up being spread so thin that we are mediocre in everything and excellent in nothing.

There is one guaranteed formula for failure, and that is to try to please everyone.

There is a difference between something that is good and something that is right. Oftentimes, it is a challenge for many people to discern that which is good from that which is right. As Christians, our higher responsibility is always to do the right things. These come first. We should do the things that we're called to do, the things that are right, with excellence, first — before we start diversifying into other areas.

There comes a time in every person's life when he must learn to say no to many good ideas. In fact, the more an individual grows, the more opportunities he will have to say no. Becoming focused is a key to results. Perhaps no other virtue is so overlooked as a key to growth and success. The temptation is always to do a little bit of everything.

Saying no to a good idea doesn't always mean never. No may mean not right now.

There is power in the word *no*. No is an anointed word, one which can break the yoke of overcommitment and weakness. No can be used to turn a situation from bad to good, from wrong to right. Saying no can free you from burdens that you really don't need to carry right now.

It can also allow you to devote the correct amount of attention and effort to God's priorities in your life.

I'm sure that as you read the title of this nugget, past experiences and present situations come to mind. I'm sure you recall many situations in which no or not right now would have been the right answer. Don't put yourself through that kind of disappointment in the future.

Yes and no are the two most important words that you will ever say. These are the two words that determine your destiny in life. How and when you say them affects your entire future.

Saying no to lesser things can mean saying yes to the priorities in your life.

D~AY~ 20

WHEN YOU REFUSE TO CHANGE, YOU END UP IN CHAINS.

We humans are custom-built for change.

Inanimate objects like clothes, houses, and buildings don't have the ability to truly change. They grow out of style and become unusable. But at any point in time, at any age, any one of us is able to change. To change doesn't always mean to do the opposite. In fact, most of the time, it means to add on to or slightly adjust.

When we are called upon by the Lord to change, we will continue to reach toward the same goal, but perhaps in a slightly different way. When we refuse to cooperate with the change that God is requiring of us, we make chains that constrain and restrict us.

There are three things that we know about the future: 1) it is not going to be like the past, 2) it is not going to be exactly the way we think it's going to be, and 3) the rate of change will take place faster than we imagine. The Bible indicates that in the end times in which we are now living, changes will come about much quicker than ever before in history.

In 1803 the British created a civil service position in which a man was required to stand on the cliffs of Dover with a spy glass. His job was to be on the lookout for invasion. He was to ring a bell if he saw the army of Napoleon Bonaparte approaching. Now that was all well and good for the time, but that job was not eliminated until 1945! How many spy glasses on the cliffs of Dover are we still holding onto in our lives? **We should choose not to allow "the way we've always done it" to cause us to miss opportunities God is providing for us today.**

Even the most precious of all gems needs to be chiseled and faceted to achieve its best luster. There is nothing that remains so constant as change. Don't end up like concrete, all mixed up and permanently set.

In Isaiah 42:9, the Lord declares: *Behold, the former things are come to pass, and new things do I declare: before they spring forth I tell you of them.* The Bible is a book that tells us how to respond to change ahead of time. You see, I believe that we can decide in advance how we will respond to most situations. When I was coaching basketball many years ago, I used to tell my players that most situations in a game can be prepared for ahead of time. We used to practice different game situations so that when the players got into an actual game situation they would know how to respond. **One of the main reasons the Bible was written was to prepare us ahead of time, to teach us how to respond in advance to many of the situations that we will encounter in life.**

Choose to flow with God's plan. Be sensitive to the new things He is doing. Stay flexible to the Holy Spirit and know that ours is a God who directs, adjusts, moves, and corrects us. He is always working to bring us into perfection.

DAY 21

"AN ARMY OF SHEEP LED BY A LION WOULD DEFEAT AN ARMY OF LIONS LED BY A SHEEP." — OLD ARAB PROVERB

What are the actions and attributes of a leader? What is it that makes him different from others?

1. A leader is always full of praise.

2. A leader learns to use the phrases "thank you"and "please" on his way to the top.

3. A leader is always growing.

4. A leader is possessed with his dreams.

5. A leader launches forth before success is certain.

6. A leader is not afraid of confrontation.

7. A leader talks about his own mistakes before talking about someone else's.

8. A leader is a person of honesty and integrity.

9. A leader has a good name.

10. A leader makes others better.

11. A leader is quick to praise and encourage the smallest amount of improvement.

12. A leader is genuinely interested in others.

13. A leader looks for opportunities to find someone doing something right.

14. A leader takes others up with him.

15. A leader responds to his own failures and acknowledges them before others have to discover and reveal them.

16. A leader never allows murmuring — from himself or others.

17. A leader is specific in what he expects.

18. A leaders holds accountable those who work with him.

19. A leader does what is right rather than what is popular.

20. A leader is a servant.

A leader is a lion, not a sheep.

D<small>AY</small> 22

PEOPLE ARE BORN ORIGINALS, BUT MOST DIE COPIES.

The call in your life is not a copy.

In this day of peer pressure, trends, and fads, we need to realize and accept that each person has been custom-made by God the Creator. Each of us has a unique and personal call upon our lives. We are to be our own selves and not copy other people.

Because I do a lot of work with churches, I come into contact with many different types of people. One time I talked over the phone with a pastor I had never met and who did not know me personally. We came to an agreement that I was to visit his church as a consultant. As we were closing our conversation and were setting a time to meet at the local airport, he asked me, "How will I know you when you get off the plane?"

"Oh, don't worry, pastor; I'll know you," I responded jokingly. "You all look alike."

The point of this humorous story is this: **be the person God has made YOU to be.**

The call of God upon our lives is the provision of God in our lives. We do not need to come up to the standards of anyone else. **The average person compares himself with others, but we Christians should always compare ourselves with the person God has called us to be.** That is our standard — God's unique plan and design for our lives. How the Lord chooses to deal with others has nothing to do with our individual call in life or God's timing and direction for us.

You and I can always find someone richer than we are, poorer than we are, or with more or less ability than we have. But how other people are, what they have, and what happens in their lives, has no effect upon our call. In Galatians 6:4 (TLB) we are admonished: *Let everyone be sure that he is doing his very best, for then he will have the personal satisfaction of work well done, and won't need to compare himself with someone else.*

God made you a certain way. You are unique. You are one of a kind. To copy others is to cheat yourself out of the fullness of what God has called you to be and to do.

So, choose to accept and become the person God has made you to be. Tap into the originality and creative genius of God in your life.

Day 23

STOP EVERY DAY AND LOOK AT
THE SIZE OF GOD.

Who is God? What is His personality like?
What are His character traits?

According to the Bible, He is everlasting,
just, caring, holy, divine, omniscient, omnipotent, omni-present and sovereign. He is light,
perfection, abundance, salvation, wisdom, and
love. He is the Creator, Savior, Deliverer,
Redeemer, Provider, Healer, Advocate, and
Friend. Never forget Who lives inside of you:
*...the Lord...the great God, the great King above all
gods* (Ps. 95:3 NIV).

John, the beloved disciple, tells us: *Ye are of
God, little children, and have overcome them: because
greater is he that is in you, than he that is in the world*
(1 John 4:4). Period. Exclamation point. That
settles it!

**God and the devil are not equal, just
opposite.**

I travel by air quite often and one of the
benefits is that every time I fly I get a glimpse of
God's perspective. I like looking at my challenges
from 37,000 feet in the air. **No problem is too**

large for God's intervention, and no person is too small for God's attention.

God is always able. If you don't need miracles, you don't need God. Dave Bordon, a friend of mine, said it best: "I don't understand the situation, but I understand God."

The miraculous realm of God always has to do with multiplication, not addition.

God likens our life in Him to seedtime and harvest. Do you realize how miraculous that is? Let me give you a conservative example: Suppose one kernel of corn produces one stalk with two ears, each ear having 200 kernels. From those 400 kernels come 400 stalks with 160,000 kernels. All from one kernel planted only one season earlier.

Our confession to the Lord should be Jeremiah 32:17 (NIV): "*Ah, Sovereign Lord, you have made the heavens and the earth by your great power and outstretched arm. Nothing is too hard for you.*"

God is bigger than_____
_____ . Fill in the blank for your own life.

DAY 24

RETREAT TO ADVANCE.

Sometimes the most important and urgent thing we can do is get away to a peaceful and anointed spot.

This is one of the most powerful concepts that I personally have incorporated into my life. I'm sitting right now writing this book in a cabin up on a hill overlooking a beautiful lake, miles away from the nearest city.

As we choose to draw away for a time, we can see and hear much more clearly about how to go ahead. Jesus did this many times during His earthly life, especially just before and after major decisions. The Bible says, *...in quietness and in confidence shall be your strength...*(Is. 30:15). There's something invigorating and renewing about retreating to a quiet place of rest and peace. Silence is an environment in which great ideas are birthed.

There really are times when you should not see people, times when you should direct your whole attention toward God. I believe that every person should have a place of refuge, one out of the normal scope of living, one where he can "retreat to advance" and "focus in" with just the Lord and himself.

It is important to associate intently and as often as possible with your loftiest dreams. In Isaiah 40:31 we read, *But they that wait upon the Lord shall renew their strength; they shall mount up with wings as eagles; they shall run, and not be weary; and they shall walk, and not faint.* Learn to wait upon the Lord.

Make a regular appointment with yourself; it will be one of the most important you can ever have during the course of a week or a month. Choose to retreat to advance. See how much clearer you move forward with God as a result.

DAY 25

HAVE A READY WILL AND WALK, NOT IDLE TIME AND TALK.

Acting on God's will is like riding a bicycle: if you don't go on, you go off!

Once we know God's will and timing, we should be instant to obey, taking action without delay. Delay and hesitation when God is telling us to do something now is sin. The longer we take to act on whatever God wants us to do, the more unclear His directives become. We need to make sure that we are on God's interstate highway and not in a cul-de-sac.

Ours is a God of velocity. He is a God of timing and direction. These two always go together. It is never wise to act upon only one or the other. Jumping at the first opportunity seldom leads to a happy landing. In Proverbs 25:8 the writer tells us, *Go not forth hastily to strive, lest thou know not what to do in the end thereof, when thy neighbour hath put thee to shame.* A famous saying holds that people can be divided into three groups: 1) those who make things happen, 2) those who watch things happen, and 3) those who wonder what's happening. Even the right direction taken at the wrong time is a bad decision.

Most people miss out on God's best in their lives because they're not prepared. The Bible warns us that we should be prepared continually. The Apostle Paul exhorts us: *...be instant in season, out of season...*(2 Tim. 4:2).

There is a seasonality to God. In Ecclesiastes 3:1 we read: *To every thing there is a season, and a time to every purpose under heaven.* Everything that you and I are involved in will have a spring (a time of planting and nurturing), a summer (a time of greatest growth), a fall (a time of harvest), and a winter (a time of decisions and planning).

Relax. Perceive, understand, and accept God's divine timing and direction.

DAY 26

WHEN WISDOM REIGNS, IT POURS.

We should expect wisdom to be given to us. The Bible says in James 1:5, *If any of you lack wisdom, let him ask of God, that giveth to all men liberally, and upbraideth not; and it shall be given him.*

When you have heard God's voice, you have heard His wisdom. Thank God for His powerful wisdom. It forces a passage through the strongest barriers.

Wisdom is seeing everything from God's perspective. It is knowing when and how to use the knowledge that comes from the Lord. The old saying is true, "He who knows nothing, doubts nothing." But it is also true that he who knows has a solid basis for his belief.

Just think, we human beings have available to us the wisdom of the Creator of the universe. Yet **so few drink at the fountain of His wisdom; most just rinse out their mouths.** Many may try to live without the wisdom of the bread of life, but they will die in their efforts.

The world doesn't spend billions of dollars for wisdom. It spends billions in search of wisdom. Yet it is readily available to everyone who seeks its divine source.

There are ten steps to gaining godly wisdom:

1. Fear God (Ps. 111:10)
2. Please God (Eccl. 2:26)
3. Hear God (Prov. 2:6)
4. Look to God (Prov. 3:13)
5. Choose God's way (Prov. 8:10,11)
6. Be humble before God (Prov. 11:2)
7. Take God's advice (Prov. 13:10)
8. Receive God's correction (Prov. 29:15)
9. Pray to God (Eph. 1:17)
10. Know the Son of God (1 Cor. 1:30)

D<small>AY</small> 27

HEARING TELLS YOU THAT
THE MUSIC IS PLAYING;
LISTENING TELLS YOU
WHAT THE SONG IS SAYING.

One of the least developed skills among us human beings is that of listening. There are really two different kinds of listening. There is the natural listening in interaction with other people, and there is spiritual listening to the voice of God.

It has been said, "Men are born with two ears, but only one tongue, which indicates that they were meant to listen twice as much as they talk." In natural communication, leaders always "monopolize the listening." **What we learn about another person will always result in a greater reward than what we tell him about ourselves.** We need to learn to listen and observe aggressively. We must try harder to truly listen, and not just to hear.

In regard to spiritual listening, Proverbs 8:34,35 (NIV) quotes wisdom who says:

Blessed is the man who listens to me, watching daily at my doors, waiting at my doorway.

For whoever finds me finds life and receives favor from the Lord.

There is great wisdom and favor to be gained by listening.

Proverbs 15:31 (NIV) says, *He who listens to a life-giving rebuke will be at home among the wise.* Listening allows us to maintain a teachable spirit. It increases our "teach-ability." Those who give us a life-giving rebuke can be a great blessing to us.

The Bible teaches that we are to be quick to listen and slow to speak. (James 1:19.) We must never listen passively, especially to God. If we resist hearing, a hardening can take place in our lives. Callousness can develop. In Luke 16:31 (NIV), Jesus said of a certain group of people, "…'*If they do not listen to Moses and the Prophets, they will not be convinced even if someone rises from the dead.*'" The more we resist listening to the voice of God, the more hardened and less fine-tuned our hearing becomes.

There are results of spiritual hearing, as we see in Luke 8:15 (NIV). This passage relates to the parable of the sower: "…*the seed on good soil stands for those with a noble and good heart, who hear the word, retain it, and by persevering produce a crop.*" Harvest is associated not only with persevering and good seed in good soil, but also with those people who hear the Word of God and retain it.

Fine-tune your natural and spiritual ears to listen and learn.

DAY 28

GOD IS NOT YOUR PROBLEM; GOD IS ON YOUR SIDE.

Some time ago I was eating at a Mexican fast food restaurant. As I stood in line for service I noticed in front of me a very poor elderly lady who looked like a street person. When it came her turn, she ordered some water and one taco. As I sat in the booth right next to her, I couldn't help but observe and be moved with compassion toward her. Shortly after I had begun my meal I went over to her and asked if I could buy some more food for her lunch. She looked at me and angrily asked, "Who are you?"

"Just a guy who wants to help you," I responded. She ignored me. I finished my meal about the same time she did, and we both got up to leave. I felt led to give her some money. In the parking lot I approached her and offered her some cash. Her only response to me was, "Stop bothering me." Then, she stormed off.

Immediately, the Lord showed me that this is often the way many of us respond to Him. When He calls out to us, seeking to bless us, we act as though we don't even know Who He is. We respond to His offer of blessing by asking, "Who are You? What do You want from me?"

The Lord, being the gracious God He is, continues to try to bless us. Yet we react by saying, "Stop bothering me." We walk off, just as this lady did, missing out on the rich blessings of the Lord.

It's not the absence of problems that gives us peace; it's God's presence with us in the problems. In Matthew 28:20, Jesus sent His disciples into all the world, ordering them to preach the Gospel to every creature: *Teaching them to observe all things whatsoever I have commanded you; and, lo, I am with you alway, even unto the end of the world.* In Romans 8:38,39 (NIV), the Apostle Paul writes, *For I am convinced that neither death nor life, neither angels nor demons, neither the present nor the future, nor any powers, neither height nor depth, nor anything else in all creation, will be able to separate us from the love of God that is in Christ Jesus our Lord.* In verse 31 he declares, *What, then, shall we say in response to this? If God is for us, who can be against us?* A paraphrase might be, "If God is for us, who cares who is against us?"

In Psalm 145:18 (NIV), we read, *The Lord is near to all who call on him, to all who call on him in truth.* James 4:8 (NIV) admonishes us, *Come near to God and he will come near to you.* In Acts 17:27 (NIV) Paul speaks: *"'For in him we live and move and have our being.'"*

Thank God that we can, without hesitation and with full confidence, lean on His eternal faithfulness.

DAY 29

LEARN THE ALPHABET FOR SUCCESS.

A   Action

B   Belief

C   Commitment

D   Direction

E   Enthusiasm

F   Faith

G   Goals

H   Happiness

I   Inspiration

J   Judgment

K   Knowledge

L   Love

M   Motivation

N   Nonconformity

O   Obedience

P   Persistence

Q   Quality

R   Righteousness

S   Steadfastness

T   Thankfulness

U   Uniqueness

V   Vision

W   Wisdom

X   (E)xcellence

Y   Yieldedness

Z   Zeal

DAY 30

THE MEASURE OF A MAN IS NOT WHAT HE DOES ON SUNDAY, BUT RATHER WHO HE IS MONDAY THROUGH SATURDAY.

You don't have to come out of the Spirit realm. The same closeness, strength, joy, and direction you experience on Sunday, God intends for you to walk in the rest of the week. The devil is waiting to ambush you as you leave church. He wants to bring to your mind thoughts of fear, doubt, unbelief, and destruction.

That's why we believers must guard our minds and hearts. As spiritual creatures, we walk by faith, not by sight. (2 Cor. 5:7.) We are commanded to live in the Spirit and not in the natural.

A person whose eyes, ears, and mind are directed toward the world finds it difficult to hear God speaking to him. The Lord wants to talk to you at work, at lunch, at play — everywhere you go. Some of my greatest revelations from God have come not in my prayer closet, but rather "out of the blue" in the midst of my normal, everyday life.

Our inner man is always willing, but our natural man resists. That's what Jesus meant when He said to His disciples, *Watch and pray, that ye enter not into temptation; the spirit indeed is willing, but the flesh is weak* (Matt. 26:41.)

The advantage of living and walking in the Spirit is that it keeps us on the right path. In Galatians 5:16, 17 (NIV) the Apostle Paul writes: *So I say, live by the Spirit, and you will not gratify the desire of the sinful nature. For the sinful nature desires what is contrary to the Spirit, and the Spirit what is contrary to the sinful nature. They are in conflict with each other, so that you do not do what you want. But if you are led by the Spirit, you are not under law.*

Thank God that our relationship with Him is not a "some-time affair," it's an "all-the-time union." In the words of the old hymn, "He leadeth me! O blessed thought!"

D<small>AY</small> 31

GOD WILL USE YOU RIGHT WHERE YOU ARE TODAY.

You don't need to do anything else for God to begin to use you now. You don't have to read another paperback book, listen to another cassette tape, memorize another scripture, plant another seed gift, or repeat another creed or confession. You don't even need to attend another church service before God will begin to make use of you.

God uses willing vessels, not brimming vessels. Throughout the Bible, in order to fulfill His plans for the earth, God used many people from all walks of life. He used:

1.   Matthew, a government employee, who became an apostle.

2.   Gideon, a common laborer, who became a valiant leader of men.

3.   Jacob, a deceiver, whose name became Israel.

4.   Deborah, a housewife, who became a judge.

5.   Moses, a stutterer, who became a deliverer.

6. Jeremiah, a child, who fearlessly spoke the Word of the Lord.

7. Aaron, a servant, who became God's spokesman.

8. Nicodemus, a Pharisee, who became a defender of the faith.

9. David, a shepherd boy, who became a king.

10. Hosea, a marital failure, who prophesied to save Israel.

11. Joseph, a prisoner, who became prime minister.

12. Esther, an orphan, who became a queen.

13. Elijah, a homely man, who became a mighty prophet.

14. Joshua, an assistant, who became a conqueror.

15. James and John, fishermen, who became close disciples of Christ and were known as "sons of thunder."

16. Abraham, a nomad, who became the father of many nations.

17. Peter, a businessman, who became the rock on which Christ built His Church.

18. Jacob, a refugee, who became the father of the twelve tribes of Israel.

19. John the Baptist, a vagabond, who became the forerunner of Jesus.

20. Mary, an unknown virgin, who gave birth to the Son of God.

21. Nehemiah, a cupbearer, who built the wall of Jerusalem.

22. Shadrach, Meshach, and Abednego, Hebrew exiles, who became great leaders of the nation of Babylon.

23. Hezekiah, a son of an idolatrous father, who became a king renowned for doing right in the sight of the Lord.

24. Isaiah, a man of unclean lips, who prophesied the birth of God's Messiah.

25. Paul, a persecutor, who became the greatest missionary in history and author of two-thirds of the New Testament.

All God needs to use you is all of you!

*   *   *

A FINAL WORD

Be the whole person God called you to be. Don't settle for anything less. Don't look back. Look forward and decide today to take steps toward His plan for your life.

And remember First Thessalonians 5:24: *Faithful is he that calleth you, who also will do it.*

Endnote

[1]Adapted from *An Enemy Called Average* (Tulsa: Harrison House, 1990).

Part IV
A Treasure of Quotes

Words of wisdom

The nose of the bulldog has been slanted backwards so that he can breathe without letting go.

The price of greatness is responsibility.

Winston Churchill

Nothing great will ever be achieved without great men, and men are great only if they are determined to be so.

For glory gives herself only to those who have always dreamed of her.

Charles De Gaulle

Try not to become a man of success but rather try to become a man of value.

Albert Einstein

Leadership: the art of getting someone else to do something you want done because he wants to do it.

An intellectual is a man who takes more words than necessary to tell more than he knows.

Though force can protect in emergency, only justice, fairness, consideration and cooperation can finally lead men to the dawn of eternal peace.

Dwight D. Eisenhower

Failure is only the opportunity to begin again more intelligently.

Anyone who stops learning is old, whether at twenty or eighty. Anyone who keeps learning stays young. The greatest thing in life is to keep your mind young.

My best friend is the one who brings out the best in me.

It is not the employer who pays wages — he only handles the money. It is the product that pays wages.

Don't find fault. Find a remedy.

The high wage begins down in the shop. If it is not created there it cannot get into pay envelopes. There will never be a system invented which will do away with necessity for work.

Henry Ford

Beware of little expenses. A small leak will sink a great ship.

The heart of a fool is in his mouth, but the mouth of a wise man is in his heart.

Well done is better than well said.

Benjamin Franklin

The brave man inattentive to his duty is worth little more to his country than the coward who deserts in the hour of danger.

One man with courage makes a majority.

Andrew Jackson

The most valuable of all talents is that of never using two words when one will do.

We confide in our strength, without boasting of it; we respect that of others, without fearing it.

Thomas Jefferson

A child miseducated is a child lost.

For without belittling the courage with which men have died, we should not forget those acts of courage with which men have lived.

John F. Kennedy

If a man is called to be a streetsweeper, he should sweep streets even as Michelangelo painted, or Beethoven composed music, or Shakespeare wrote poetry. He should sweep streets so well that all the hosts of heaven and earth will pause to say, here lived a great streetsweeper who did his job well.

We must use time creatively — and forever realize that the time is always hope to do great things.

Martin Luther King, Jr.

When you have got an elephant by the hind legs and he is trying to run away, it's best to let him run.

I don't think much of a man who is not wiser today than he was yesterday.

Abraham Lincoln

The quality of a person's life is in direct proportion to their commitment to excellence, regardless of their chosen field of endeavor.

It's not whether you get knocked down, it's whether you get up.

The spirit, the will to win, and the will to excel are the things that endure. These qualities are so much more important than the events that occur.

Coaches who can outline plays on a black board are a dime a dozen. The ones who win get inside their player and motivate.

Vince Lombardi

By profession I am a soldier and take pride in that fact. But I am prouder — infinitely prouder — to be a father. A soldier destroys in order to build; the father only builds, never destroys. The one has the potentiality of death; the other embodies creation and life. And while the hordes of death are mighty, the battalions of life are mightier still. It is my hope that my son, when I am gone, will remember me not from the battle but in the home repeating with him our simple daily prayer, "Our Father Who Art in Heaven."

Douglas MacArthur

Being powerful is like being a lady. If you have to tell people you are, you aren't.

Margaret Thatcher

Wars may be fought with weapons, but they are won by men. It is the spirit of the men who follow and of the man who leads that gains the victory.

Never tell people how to do things. Tell them what to do and they will surprise you with their integrity.

If everyone is thinking alike then somebody isn't thinking.

General George S. Patton

The test of our progress is not whether we add more to the abundance of those who have much; it is whether we provide enough for those who have too little.

Happiness lies in the joy of achievement and the thrill of creative effort.

There is no indispensable man.

Franklin D. Roosevelt

I think there is only one quality worse than hardness of heart and that is softness of head.

When they call the roll in the Senate, the senators do not know whether to answer "present" or "not guilty."

The best executive is the one who has sense enough to pick good men to do what he wants done, and self-restraint enough to keep from meddling with them while they do it.

Theodore Roosevelt

I learned that a great leader is a man who has the ability to get other people to do what they don't want to do and like it.

It's a recession when your neighbor loses his job; it's a depression when you lose your own.

Harry S. Truman

Excellence is to do a common thing in an uncommon way.

The world cares very little about what a man or woman knows; it is what the man or woman is able to do that counts.

You can't hold a man down without staying down with him.

Booker T. Washington

Discipline is the soul of an army. It makes small numbers formidable, procures success to the weak, and esteem to all.

If the freedom of speech is taken away then dumb and silent we may be led, like sheep to the slaughter.

George Washington

Do not let what you cannot do interfere with what you can do.

Failure to prepare is preparing to fail.

Sports do not build character. They reveal it.

Be more concerned with your character than with your reputation. Your character is what you really are while your reputation is merely what others think you are.

John Wooden

No one is useless in this world who lightens the burden of it to anyone else.

Charles Dickens

Give me a stock clerk with a goal, and I will give you a man who will make history. Give me a man without a goal, and I will give you a stock clerk.

J. C. Penney

What lies behind us and what lies before us are tiny matters compared to what lies within us.

For the resolute and determined there is time and opportunity.

Ralph Waldo Emerson

In order to succeed, you must know what you are doing, like what you are doing and believe in what you are doing.

Will Rogers

Winners will take care of themselves. When you give your best effort, that is what makes you a winner.

There is no limit to what can be accomplished when no one cares who gets the credit.

John Wooden

Success. . . seems to be connected with action. Successful people keep moving. They make mistakes, but they don't quit.

Conrad Hilton

Surely a man has come to himself only when he has found the best that is in him, and has satisfied his heart with the highest achievement he is fit for.

Woodrow Wilson

You get the best out of others when you give the best of yourself.

Harvey Firestone

Destiny is not a matter of chance, it is a matter of choice.

Anonymous

The future belongs to those who believe in the beauty of their dreams.

Eleanor Roosevelt

Accept the challenges, so that you may feel that exhilaration of victory.

General George S. Patton

As I grow older, I pay less attention to what men say. I just watch what they do.

Andrew Carnegie

The credit belongs to the man who is actually in the arena, whose face is marred by dust and sweat and blood; who strives valiantly; who errs and comes short again and again, who knows the great enthusiasms, the great devotions, and spends himself in a worthy cause; who at the best, knows the triumph of high achievement; and who, at the worst, if he fails, at least fails while daring greatly, so that his place shall never be with those cold and timid souls who know neither victory nor defeat.

Theodore Roosevelt

Nothing in the world can take the place of persistence.

Talent will not; nothing is more common than unsuccessful men with talent. Genius will not; unrewarded genius is almost a proverb.

Education will not; the world is full of educated derelicts.

Persistence and determination alone are omnipotent.

Calvin Coolidge

Failure is the opportunity to begin again more intelligently.

Henry Ford

Without passion man is a mere latent force and a possibility, like the flint which awaits the shock of the iron before it can give forth its spark.

Henri Frederic Ameil

There are many things that will catch my eye, but there are only a very few that catch my heart...it is those I consider to pursue.

Tim Redmond

The average man does not know what to do with this life, yet wants another one which will last forever.

Anatold France

Not doing more than the average is what keeps the average down.

William M. Winans

Of all the sad words of tongue or pen, the saddest are these: It might have been!

John Greenleaf Whittier

Don't be content to be the chip off the old block, be the old block itself.

Winston Churchill

It's a funny thing about life; if you refuse to accept anything but the best, you very often get it.

Somerset Maugham

Don't let your learning lead to knowledge, let your learning lead to action.

Jim Rohn

An invasion of armies can be resisted, but not an idea whose time has come.

Victor Hugo

The greatest thing in this world is not so much where we are, but in what direction we are moving.

Oliver Wendell Holmes

It has been my observation that most people get ahead during the time that others waste.

Henry Ford

Find something you love to do and you'll never have to work another day in your life.

Harvey Mackay

For all your days prepare, and meet them ever alike: when you are the anvil, bear — when you are the hammer, strike.

Edwin Markham

Waste your money and you're only out of money but waste your time and you've lost a part of your life.

Michael Leboeuf

The highest reward for man's toil is not what he gets for it but what he becomes by it.

Ruskin

Don't just make a living; design a life.

Jim Rohn

The poorest man is not he who is without a cent, but he who is without a dream.

Pennsylvania School Journal

What counts is not necessarily the size of the dog in the fight — it's the size of the fight in the dog.

D. Eisenhower

Show me someone who has done something worthwhile, and I'll show you someone who has overcome adversity.

Lou Holtz

Age may wrinkle the face, but lack of enthusiasm wrinkles the soul.

Anonymous

What It Takes To Be No. 1

Winning is not a sometime thing; it's an all the time thing. You don't win once in a while; you don't do things right once in a while; you do them right all the time. Winning is a habit. Unfortunately, so is losing.

There is no room for second place. There is only one place in my game, and that's first place. I have finished second twice in my time at Green Bay, and I don't ever want to finish second again. There is a second place bowl game, but it is a game for losers played by losers. It is and always has been an American zeal to be first in anything we do, and to win, and to win, and to win.

Every time a football player goes to ply his trade he's got to play from the ground up — from the soles of his feet right up to his head. Every inch of him has to play. Some guys play with their heads. That's O.K. You've got to play with your heart, with every fiber of your body. If you're lucky enough to find a guy with a lot of head and a lot of heart, he's never going to come off the field second.

Running a football team is no different than running any other kind of organization — an army, a political party or business. The principles are the same. The object is to win — to beat the other guy. Maybe that sounds hard or cruel. I don't think it is.

It is a reality of life that men are competitive and the most competitive games draw the most competitive men. That's why they are there — to compete. To know the rules and objectives when they get in the game. The object is to win fairly, squarely, by the rules — but to win.

And in truth, I've never known a man worth his salt who in the long run, deep down in his heart, didn't appreciate the grind, the discipline. There is something in good men that really yearns for discipline and the harsh reality of head to head combat.

I don't say these things because I believe in the "brute" nature of man or that men must be brutalized to be combative. I believe in God, and I believe in human decency. But I firmly believe that any man's finest hour — his greatest fulfillment to all he holds dear — is that moment when he has to work his heart out in a good cause and he's exhausted on the field of battle — victorious.

Vincent Lombardi

If—

If you can keep your head when all about you
    Are losing theirs and blaming it on you;

If you can trust yourself when all men doubt you,
    But make allowance for their doubting too;

If you can wait and not be tired by waiting,
    Or, being lied about, don't deal in lies,

Or, being hated, don't give way to hating,
    And yet don't look too good, nor talk too wise;

If you can dream — and not make dreams your
        master;
    If you can think — and not make thoughts
        your aim;

If you can meet with triumph and disaster
    And treat those two impostors just the same;

If you can bear to hear the truth you've spoken
    Twisted by knaves to make a trap for fools,

Or watch the things you gave your life to
        broken,
    And stoop and build 'em up with wornout
        tools;

If you can make one heap of all your winnings
    And risk it on one turn of pitch-and-toss,

And lose, and start again at your beginnings
    And never breathe a word about your loss;

If you can force your heart and nerve and sinew
    To serve your turn long after they are gone,

And so hold on when there is nothing in you
    Except the Will which says to them: "Hold on";

If you can talk with crowds and keep your
     virtue,
    Or walk with kings nor lose the common
       touch;
If neither foes nor loving friends can hurt you;
    If all men count with you, but none too
      much;
If you can fill the unforgiving minute
    With sixty seconds' worth of distance run —
Yours is the Earth and everything that's in it,
    And — which is more — you'll be a Man,
      my son!

                       Rudyard Kipling

PRAYER FOR SALVATION

Father, I pray to You and I know that I am a sinner. I need Jesus Christ in my life to save me from my sins. Thank You that You love me in spite of the type of person I have been or the things that I have done.

The Bible says that all have sinned and come short of the glory of God. It also says that my salvation is a gift from You to me. Your grace with faith is what saves me, not anything I can do or say. I confess my sins; You are faithful to forgive my sins and cleanse me from all unrighteousness and wrongful behavior. (1 John 1:9.) I turn my back on the devil and will strive to be the person that Jesus wants me to be.

Your Word says if I say with my mouth that Jesus is Lord and believe in my heart that You raised Him from the dead, I will be saved. (Rom. 10:9,10.) Jesus, I say out loud that You are the Lord of my life, and I believe that God raised You from the dead. Thank You that You are the Lord over every area of my life — my thoughts, my actions and my relationships.

Thank You, Father, for saving me! I am a new person in Jesus Christ, and heaven is my home for eternity. I recognize that I am saved by faith and not by emotion. Jesus, You are my friend, especially when I am going through hard times. As long as I stay faithful to You, no problem is too great for me.

Father, You said that I have the mind of Christ. (1 Corinthians 2:16.) I pray now for a clear mind to learn more about You. I pray that I will grow strong in my faith toward You and Your Son, Jesus. I want to know all I can about You so that I can share Your love and salvation with my friends and other people I know. Thank You, Lord, for saving me!

Van Crouch is widely regarded as one of the best and more versatile speakers in America.

As the founder and president of the consulting firm, Van Crouch Communications, Van challenges individuals to achieve excellence in their lives.

Van's experiences in the corporate arena and as a speaker to many of the nation's professional sports teams, give him an enthusiasm for life, a spontaneous sense of humor and a genuine interest in people.

After ranking as a consistent sales leader with the American Express Company, Van went on to receive many awards for outstanding performance in the insurance industry and has been a qualifying member of the Million Dollar Roundtable.

Van Crouch authored the best-selling book, *Stay in the Game.*

Van is in demand for his thought-provoking seminars and keynote engagements to Fortune 500 companies, government organizations, church groups and management and sales conventions worldwide.

Van's seminars cover a range of topics:

Destined To Win
On the Growing Edge
Developing Competitive Excellence
Get It Done Now
The Hour of Sales Power
Grow Toward Leadership

Van Crouch has the ability to motivate people to raise their level of expectation. He will cause your attitude to become more positive, your problems smaller, your self-esteem and confidence will grow and your self-doubts disintegrate. He is sure to both inspire and challenge you.

Currently, Van and his wife, Doni, live in Wheaton, Illinois.

For more information about Van Crouch's seminars, speaking engagements, cassette tapes and videos, write:

Van Crouch Communications
P. O. Box 320
Wheaton, IL 60187